Paul

Forrestal

FOOD WITH FLAIR

FOOD WITH FLAIR

Sue Lawrence

Foreword by

LOYD GROSSMAN

MAINSTREAM
PUBLISHING

EDINBURGH AND LONDON

First published in Great Britain in 1993 by
MAINSTREAM PUBLISHING COMPANY
(EDINBURGH) LTD
7 Albany Street
Edinburgh EH1 3UG

ISBN 1 85158 559 1

A catalogue record for this book is available from the
British Library

Typeset in Monophoto Baskerville by
Servis Filmsetting Ltd, Manchester

Printed by Mandarin Offset Ltd, Hong Kong

Photography by Victor Albrow
Calligraphy by Joi Lynda Millgate
Design by James Hutcheson

Contents

37

THREE

Butter-bean and Herb Salad; Olive Oil Bread;
Sea Bass with Red Pepper and Basil Sauce; Spinach with Sorrel
Strawberry and Cream Cheese Ice-Cream
Rick Stein of The Seafood Restaurant: Roast Sea Bass with Red Cabbage
and Rosti Potatoes

47

FOUR

Pasta with Brie and Fennel
Beef with Herb Crust; Roast Parsnips; Glazed Shallots
Lemon Curd Bread and Butter Pudding
Anthony Tobin of South Lodge Hotel: Fresh Ravioli of Langoustine with
Sweet Peppers and its own Vinaigrette

61

FIVE

Jerusalem Artichoke and Smoked Haddock Soup
Cod with Rosemary; Ratatouille Mounds
Dark Treacle Ice-Cream with Lemon Shortbread
Gary Rhodes of The Greenhouse: Fillet of Cod on Mashed Potato with a
Lentil and Mustard Sauce

71

SIX

Pickled Herring in Seaweed; Rye Bread Rolls
Rack of Lamb with Mint Pesto; Mushroom and Potato Ramekins
Hazelnut and Chocolate Fudge Tart
Christopher Chown of Plas Bodegroes: Roast Best End of Lamb with
Mustard and Peppers

81

SEVEN

Kipper Fish-cakes with Avocado Sauce
Mussels in a Chilli Sauce; Barley Bread
Mincemeat Shortcake with Apricots
Antony Worrall Thompson of 190 Queen's Gate and dell'Ugo: Steamed
Mussels with Coriander, Greens and Lentil Broth

93
EIGHT
Langoustines with Lemon Grass Mayonnaise
Chicken with Feta and Tomatoes; Pasta with Rocket
Blackcurrant Tart
Betty Allen of The Airds Hotel: Chicken Breasts filled with Mushrooms

103
NINE
Mussels in Buckwheat Crêpes
Oxtail with Gremolata; Celeriac Purée
Steamed Ginger and Pear Pudding
David Adlard of Adlard's Restaurant: Apple Charlotte and
Cinnamon Ice-Cream

115
TEN
Warm Artichoke Bread with Tomato Salad
Fresh Pasta with Wild Mushrooms and Cream
Quince Compote
Paul Rankine of Roscoff Restaurant: Pappardelle with Artichokes,
Girolles and a Basil Pesto

125
ELEVEN
Warm Goat's Cheese Salad
Rabbit with Black Olive Paste; Braised Borlotti Beans
Bramble Clafoutis
John Tovey of Miller Howe: Trio of Salmon

135
TWELVE
Smoked Venison with Melon
Herring Gratin; Green Salad with Garlic Vinaigrette
Tablet and Fruits in Season
Alastair Little of Alastair Little's Restaurant: Grilled and Marinated
Herring

Acknowledgments

I MUST EXTEND MY THANKS TO THE CHEFS WHO VERY KINDLY TOOK THE time, from their hectic routines, to contribute a recipe to this book. I am extremely grateful to Anne Dow for her invaluable help, recipe testing and food styling; to Ian Breslin and his assistant Gavin Borthwick at Armstrongs Fishmongers, Raeburn Place, Edinburgh, for their consistently excellent seafood; to Robert Wilson of Scotherbs, Errol, for supplying his wonderful fresh herbs; to Jenners, Princes Street, Edinburgh, for their use of crockery and materials for photography; and to Emma Bridgewater Ltd, Fulham Road, London, for their charming pottery.

Notes on Measurements and Serving Numbers

Metric and imperial measurements are given to their nearest rounded equivalent. Results will be satisfactory only when one set of measurements is adhered to. To use American cup measurements, an approximate conversion is 1 cup to 250ml/8 fl oz.

Unless otherwise stated, the eggs used are always size 3.

Teaspoons and tablespoons are always level, unless indicated otherwise, 1 tsp = 5 ml; 1 tbsp = 15 ml.

All recipes serve 4, unless otherwise specified.

Foreword

From the first time I tasted Sue Lawrence's cooking I was full of admiration for it. So were my fellow judges and Sue of course went on to win the title of BBC Masterchef 1991. Since then, the programme's production team and I have been thrilled and gratified to see Sue establish herself as a really first-rate cookery writer. I feel sure that this book will add further to her sparkling reputation.

I tend to divide cooks into the traditionalists and the innovators. They each have their own set of problems. The traditionalist's pitfall is boredom and predictability while the innovators may get into a tiresome routine of change for change's sake. Sue is one of the innovators, but she keeps away from what I call 'loony inventiveness' by being so firmly rooted in the theory and practice of real, old-fashioned eating. This book is bursting with good ideas and alluring fancies, but they sit on a bedrock of great ingredients and vivid flavours. Perhaps most importantly, these pages testify to a rollicking and unpretentious love of food that should send all cooks scampering towards their kitchens.

Loyd Grossman
London, 1993

Introduction

BRITISH FOOD HAS BEEN MUCH MALIGNED OVER THE YEARS. IT HAS BEEN over-cooked, often destroying the natural flavours; it has been over-processed, thereby removing healthy nutrients and encouraging an appetite for blandness; and it has been served with indifference, rather than with respect and pride. Since we have such fine natural produce all over the British Isles, it is a joy to witness the advent, over the past couple of decades, of quality British cooking and a return to the use of unadulterated natural produce.

The seasons, which used to be fundamental in one's choice of ingredients, are often completely ignored nowadays, because of freezers and air-freighting. I feel strongly that the thrilling taste of the first strawberry of summer, or the fragrant smell of raspberry jam being made one month later, or the wonderful sight of the first Cox apples on the trees in early autumn, should not become fading memories. Seasons are important because food, on the whole, tastes better fresh. (Although, like many others, I could not do without my freezer, I try to use it only for glut produce, or batch-baking and cooking.) I remember when I lived in Finland, watching the Finns go round Helsinki's market at midsummer time. Not usually given to demonstrative behaviour, they were impatiently tasting the new summer produce: strawberries, fresh peas or dill were bought and tasted at once with that enthusiasm reserved for greeting long-lost friends.

As a mother of three young children, I am aware that food should not only be nutritious, but also interesting and fun. The ready-prepared convenience meals, so often eaten by children nowadays, can surely instil in them nothing but indifference towards food. For it is merely heated up or – packaging removed – plated up and served, with as much passion as is usually displayed when putting petrol into the car. How can children learn to respect and appreciate good food if they never see it actually being cooked in their kitchens?

The simplicity of a recipe for the domestic cook is important. It makes him or her aware that home-cooked food is not only tastier, but it can also be quicker to produce than reheating a pre-cooked meal. My recipes are always easy to follow and they use good-quality produce, which is by no means expensive. They use primarily local British ingredients, supplemented by some of the vast range of interesting foreign imports which are becoming part of our culinary way of life nowadays.

I have suggested full 3-course menus, as balancing a menu is such an important part of cooking – both for entertaining friends or for everyday cooking for the family. I have given tips for advance preparation and suggestions for wine. As we are more nutritionally aware now than some years ago, there is a common theme in the book: healthy eating (in moderation!), with an emphasis on salads, fresh herbs, seafood, light sauces and home-made breads. The glorious, indulgent exceptions to this are my favourite pudding recipes, which I share with you on the strict understanding that they are, of course, only for treats!

I am indebted to the 18 chefs who very kindly contributed a recipe each. Through their dedication and hard work, these top chefs have become catalysts in the progress, albeit slow, towards gastronomic excellence, for which Britain has not, until now, been famous. There is, however, an ever-changing, exciting culinary upsurge throughout Britain. By getting back to basics – using top-quality ingredients, cooking delicious, interesting food with enthusiasm and respect – our chefs will continue to earn well-deserved plaudits from all over the world; and home cooks will continue to appreciate the pleasures of sharing meals together and how easy it is to cook food with flair.

One

THIS MENU APPEALS NOT ONLY TO THE TASTEBUDS, BUT ALSO THE EYE.
There is little to beat the sight of a perfectly risen soufflé wobbling to
the table. Few people realise that there is no mystery about making a
perfect soufflé; it is all a matter of measuring exactly and waiting patiently.
This one is flavoured with smoky roast garlic and a strong-tasting cheddar.
An interim salad of rocket and a few edible flowers is colourful, delicious
and usually a great talking-point. The main course is a risotto cooked with
juniper berries and mushrooms, then topped with quickly cooked chicken
livers. This is followed by a redcurrant sorbet, which is a glorious pink
colour and, although there is not a hint of fattening cream, its texture is rich
and creamy.

To roast garlic, you can either separate the cloves (but do not peel
them), or roast the whole head, having cut off the top to expose the open
cloves. Add some oil and roast in a hot oven until they are golden brown. In
my pre-garlic days I remember being astounded at a French friend cooking
three whole heads of plump garlic in a chicken dish. After I had squeezed
out and enjoyed my eighth or ninth clove from its casing, I realised that my
misconceptions about garlic had been due to eating too many dishes
redolent of harsh, raw garlic. Garlic cloves can be roasted alongside a joint
of meat, as a change from the potatoes and parsnips. If you roast them in a
good olive oil, you also acquire garlic-flavoured oil, which you can then use
as a cooking medium, or for tossing into freshly cooked pasta. Be sure the
cheese you choose for the soufflé is mature (I like Isle of Mull Cheddar); you
need a strong flavour to counterbalance the sweet smokiness of the roasted
garlic, which, by the way, does not linger on the breath. The important
thing to remember about a soufflé as a starter is to seat people at least ten
minutes before it is due to come out of the oven. Your guests will happily
wait – the soufflé cannot.

The risotto is flecked with mushrooms – I favour strongly flavoured
ones such as shiitake or chestnut, unless you are lucky enough to obtain wild
ones, such as ceps (porcini). The risotto is flavoured with juniper berries.

Menu

Garlic and Cheddar Soufflé

Chicken Liver & Mushroom Risotto
Salad of Rocket and Flowers

Redcurrant Sorbet

These go perfectly with the chicken livers, which top the lot. Juniper berries vary considerably in strength, so you must keep tasting the risotto to see if you quickly need to crush a few more. If, by the time you have crushed 30 berries, you find yourself reaching for the tonic water, do not be surprised: juniper oil (obtained from ripe berries) is a prime flavouring in gin. The best way to crush them is in a pestle and mortar. The texture of risotto should be moist and creamy, but the individual grains of rice still rather firm. The cooking liquid (usually stock or wine) should be added a little at a time, so it can be absorbed slowly. The time to stop adding liquid is when the rice still has a little bite in it, yet is tender. I like to cook the chicken livers fiercely, and therefore separately from the rice, so they remain crunchy outside and soft and pink inside, in contrast to the rice.

The salad can be served after the first or second course. Rocket, which tastes piquant and nutty, is an excellent base for edible flowers in a salad. Use heartsease (a member of the viola family) – they taste mildly sweet. Nasturtium flowers taste peppery and spicy; the leaves have an even more pungent, almost cress-like taste, and they are also good in salads. Marigold petals (often used as a poor man's saffron) are slightly bitter and aromatic. Any of these flowers, as well as many herb flowers such as rocket, thyme, sage or chive flowers, should be added to a salad at the last minute. The dressing should be simple and light, otherwise the delicate flowers will wilt.

The bold pink redcurrant sorbet provides the perfect ending to this visual feast. Its flavour is slightly tart; its texture full and creamy, although it is made only from currants, sugar and egg whites . . . with just a suggestion of gin (just in case you are still dreaming of that long cool drink).

ADVANCE PREPARATION

The garlic can be roasted in advance, but the soufflé must be baked at the last minute. The risotto must also be cooked just before serving. The vinaigrette can be made several hours before, but should not be tossed into the salad until you are ready to eat. The sorbet is best eaten on the day it is made.

WINE SUGGESTIONS

For the first two courses try a good Australian Cabernet Sauvignon wine from the Coonawarra district (Hardy, Penfolds, Rosemount and Wynns are names to look for). Moscato Piemonte Spumante, or another sweet, perfumed, sparkling wine, will go well with the sorbet.

Garlic and Cheddar Soufflé

1 large head of garlic (about 50 g/2 oz)
1 tbsp olive oil
50 g/2 oz butter
40 g/1½ oz plain flour
150 ml/5 fl oz milk
150 ml/5 fl oz double cream
4 eggs, plus the white of 1 large egg
125 g/4 oz mature cheddar, grated
½ tsp Dijon mustard
salt, pepper
1 tbsp freshly grated parmesan

1. Preheat the oven to Gas 7/220°C/425°F. To roast the garlic, using a very sharp knife, cut off the top quarter of the head of garlic (to expose the cloves). Place the head in the centre of a piece of foil and drizzle over the oil. Enclose completely with the foil, then place on a baking tray and roast in the oven for about 30 minutes, until the cloves are tender. Lower the oven to Gas 5/190°C/375°F.

2. Meanwhile, make the sauce: melt the butter in a saucepan, then stir in the flour and cook for 1 minute. Add the milk and cream and cook, whisking all the time, until it becomes thick (cook for about 2–3 minutes). Remove from the heat and stir in the egg yolks, cheddar, half the parmesan, mustard and salt and pepper.

3. Once the garlic is cool enough to handle, squeeze out the garlic pulp from the skins. Add them to the sauce and blend well. (I like to use a hand-held blender.)

4. Whisk the egg whites until they are thick, but not dry.

5. Fold in a spoonful of these to the sauce, to loosen the mixture, then gently fold in the rest, until well mixed.

6. Butter a 1.2 litre/2 pint soufflé dish then sprinkle the remaining parmesan into the base, and tip it around the sides. Pour the mixture into the dish, then place in the middle of the oven and bake for about 35– 40 minutes, until well risen and golden. Serve at once.

NONE OF THE STARTER CAN BE FROZEN

Chicken Liver and Mushroom Risotto

25 g/1 oz butter
3 tbsp olive oil
1 onion, peeled, finely chopped
1 garlic clove, peeled, crushed
375 g/12 oz mushrooms, wiped, sliced
the grated zest of 1 lemon
20–30 dried juniper berries, crushed
salt, pepper
375 g/12 oz arborio (risotto) rice
300 ml/10 fl oz dry white wine
750–900 ml/1$\frac{1}{4}$–1$\frac{1}{2}$ pints hot chicken stock
500 g/1 lb chicken livers, trimmed
25–40 g/1–1$\frac{1}{2}$ oz freshly grated parmesan

1. Heat the butter and 1 tbsp of the oil in a large heavy saucepan and gently fry the onion and garlic for 2–3 minutes.

2. Add the mushrooms, lemon zest, half the juniper berries, salt and pepper and fry for another 2–3 minutes.

3. Add the rice, stirring to coat with the fat, then increase the heat and add the wine. Cook for a couple of minutes, then lower the heat. Gradually add the stock (ladle by ladle) and cook over a low heat until the rice is just tender and the stock absorbed. (This will take about 20 minutes altogether.) Stir frequently, or it will stick. (Taste to see if you need more juniper berries.)

4. Meanwhile, towards the end of cooking time, heat the remaining oil in a large frying pan until it is very hot. Add the chicken livers and the remaining juniper berries and cook over a high heat (beware – they will splatter) for 2–3 minutes, until the livers are well browned, but still pink inside.

5. To serve, check the risotto for salt and pepper, then stir in most of the parmesan. Serve on to warmed plates or shallow soup plates. Top with the chicken livers, pouring over the juices from the pan (which will be flavoured with the juniper berries). Sprinkle over the remaining parmesan and serve at once.

Salad of Rocket and Flowers

2 handfuls of washed salad leaves such as
    watercress, lettuce or young spinach
2 handfuls of rocket, washed
1 handful of edible flowers such as heartsease,
    nasturtiums, marigold petals and herb flowers,
    all picked over carefully (wash only if absolutely
    essential)

FOR THE DRESSING

2 tbsp sunflower oil
2 tbsp extra virgin olive oil
1 tbsp balsamic vinegar
salt, pepper

1. If the salad leaves are large, tear them roughly; place them, with the rocket, in a large salad bowl. Add most of the flowers.

2. Whisk together all the dressing ingredients and pour over the salad. Toss well, then decorate with the remaining flowers. Serve at once.

NONE OF THE MAIN COURSE CAN BE FROZEN

Redcurrant Sorbet

500 g/1 lb redcurrants
125 g/4 oz icing sugar, sifted
the juice of 1 lemon
2–3 drops of gin
1 large egg white

1. Place the redcurrants, sugar and lemon juice in a saucepan. Bring to the boil and simmer for 5 minutes. Remove from the heat, drain briefly (reserving the liquid), then place the fruit in a food processor, to purée.

2. Push the mixture through a sieve, then add the gin. Add about 2–3 tbsp of the reserved liquid: sufficient to give the purée the consistency of pouring cream.

3. Whisk the egg white until it is stiff, then fold it carefully into the purée.

4. Pour the mixture into a sorbet or ice-cream machine to churn until frozen (or place in the freezer, in a bowl, and beat every half hour).

5. To serve, remove from the freezer 10–15 minutes before you are ready and serve in spoonfuls on chilled plates.

ALBERT ROUX needs little introdution. With his brother Michel he has not only been mentor to many of the top chefs in Britain, he has also brought *haute cuisine* to the general public, through their television programme and their books. Albert started as a 14-year-old apprentice at Pâtisserie Leclerc, Paris. He then cooked in private households for 14 years, before he opened Le Gavroche (then in Lower Sloane Street) in 1967 with Michel. In 1981 Le Gavroche was moved to its present location in Upper Brook Street. Now Albert is joint owner of Le Gavroche with his son, Michel Jr (his brother now owns The Waterside at Bray); he oversees many of the Roux brothers' food-related operations; and he has a consultancy practice, which advises many internationally known clients from different areas of the food and hospitality industry.

(Martin Brigdale)

It is a great privilege to share one of Albert Roux's favourite recipes:

Soufflé Suissesse

(A recipe by Albert Roux,
Maître Cuisinier de France)

140 g/5 oz butter
65 g/2 oz flour
700 ml/28 fl oz milk
5 egg yolks
1 litre/1¾ pints double cream
6 egg whites
200 g/7 oz grated Gruyère or Emmenthal cheese
salt
freshly ground white pepper

1. Preheat the oven to Gas 6/200°C/400°F.

2. Melt 65 g/2 oz butter in a small saucepan set over low heat. Using a small wire whisk, stir in the flour. Cook gently for 2–3 minutes, stirring continuously.

3. Take the pan off the heat and leave the roux to cool slightly. Bring the milk to the boil, then pour it over the cooled roux, whisking all the time. Set the pan over high heat and, stirring continuously, bring the mixture to the boil and cook for 3 minutes.

4. Take the pan off the heat and stir in the egg yolks. Season to taste with salt and pepper. Dot the surface with 1 tbsp butter, cut into small pieces, to prevent a skin forming. Set aside at room temperature.

5. Meanwhile, chill 8 round 8 cm/3inch tartlet tins in the refrigerator or freezer for a few minutes. Remove and immediately grease them generously with softened butter and arrange on a baking sheet.

6. Pour the cream into a gratin or bi-metal dish. Lightly salt the cream, then warm it gently without letting it boil. Beat the egg whites with a pinch of salt until they form stiff peaks. Pour the soufflé mixture into a wide-mouthed bowl. Using a whisk, quickly beat in about one-third of the beaten egg whites, then, using a spatula, carefully fold in the remainder. Using a tablespoon, heap up the mixture in the tartlet tins to form 8 large mounds.

7. Bake the soufflés in the preheated oven for 3 minutes, until the tops begin to turn golden. Remove from the oven and, protecting your hands with a cloth, turn out each soufflé into the dish of warm cream. Sprinkle over the Gruyère or Emmenthal and return to the oven for 5 minutes.

8. The soufflés must be taken immediately to the table; serve them with a spoon and fork, taking care not to crush them.

Two

THIS MENU IS IDEAL FOR THE AUTUMN, WHEN WILD VENISON IS AVAILABLE (although the quality of farmed venison is consistently high throughout the year). Also, there are butternut squashes to be found alongside the pumpkins for Hallowe'en; and plums and sloes are in their prime.

The soup to start this warming meal has a beautiful green colour and just a hint of cumin and coriander. Potatoes and butternut squash give the soup body – the latter I came across in Australia, where they were used in many ways, just like pumpkins. They were grated into breads and scones, minced into a ravioli filing, roasted around a joint of meat, puréed and mixed with olive oil and butter, or made into gratins with strongly flavoured cheese. It is easy to obtain the pear-shaped butternut squash in this country now; their flesh is a vivid orange colour and it is firm and sweet. The spinach should be added at the very end, otherwise – instead of a beautiful bright green – the colour will be dull. If frozen spinach is used, it won't look quite as impressive, although the flavour will be the same. A slice of granary and nut bread is perfect with the soup. I prefer using hazelnuts, but walnuts or pecans are also good.

The main course was inspired by a dish I tasted at Italian friends' who live in Edinburgh. In their home town of Milan, the partnership of bland polenta is often found with rich game dishes, particularly rabbit, quail or venison. As a vegetarian alternative, the polenta can be matched with the mushroom sauce, on its own. Polenta is a coarsely ground cornmeal which traditionally takes about 40 minutes to cook, while being constantly stirred – presumably by very muscular arms. The cheat's way is to buy a packet of 'quick' polenta, which is ready in 5–10 minutes. To accompany the venison, add only butter at the end; for other polenta dishes, add olive oil or a cheese such as parmesan, fontina or gorgonzola.

The venison is coated in olive oil and roughly crushed black peppercorns, then browned all over before cooking for a short time in a hot oven. Since venison is a very lean meat, it should never be cooked to the 'well-done' stage or it would be dry and tough. The importance of the

Menu

Butternut Squash & Spinach Soup
Granary and Nut Bread

Venison with Mushrooms & Polenta

Plums in Sloe Gin

resting time for venison should not be underestimated: as the meat rests, the heat travels back towards the centre and therefore ensures even cooking and the most tender meat. Larger joints such as sirloin or haunch can also be roasted and accompanied by the mushroom sauce. When you use truffle oil, ensure it is an extra virgin oil and only use a minimal amount – it is powerful stuff! I like to serve a green salad, tossed in an oil and lemon vinaigrette, after the main course.

Plums and sloes are from the same botanical family, and are perfectly matched in this simple dessert. Plums should be firm to the touch with a bloom on the skin. Since they are high in pectin, they are excellent for mixing with other fruits lower in pectin (such as brambles or elderberries) for an autumn jam or jelly. Sloes are the fruit of the blackthorn and make a most wonderful drink, by simply pricking them all over and placing in a large jar with gin and sugar. This should be sealed and left for a couple of months (shaken every day, to let the flavours combine) then strained into a clean bottle. If you pick the sloes in October, the gin should be just about ready for Christmas. The plums, once cooked, can be served warm or cold, preferably with a good spoonful of thick clotted cream, to mix into those wonderfully alcoholic juices.

ADVANCE PREPARATION

The soup can be prepared in advance, but it is better to add the spinach at the last minute, for a vivid colour. The mushroom sauce can be prepared before and reheated, but only add the truffle oil as you serve. The plums can be cooked the day before and chilled in the fridge.

WINE SUGGESTIONS

If you plan to serve a dry sherry before the meal, encourage your guests to take their glasses to the table for the first course. Otherwise, serve Châteauneuf-du-Pape right from the start, if you are feeling extravagant; less expensive, but equally well suited to the venison, is a Shiraz from Australia's Hunter Valley. To finish, you may wish to reinforce the alcohol in the pudding with some more Sloe Gin; alternatively, serve Muscat de Beaumes de Venise.

Butternut Squash and Spinach Soup

1 tbsp olive oil
25 g/1 oz butter
1 onion, peeled, chopped
2 large potatoes (about 500 g/1 lb before peeling),
    peeled, diced
1 tsp freshly ground cumin
1 tsp freshly ground coriander
1 large butternut squash (about 1.1 kg/2½ lb before
    peeling)
250 g/8 oz fresh young leaf spinach, washed
salt, pepper

TO SERVE

thick Greek yoghurt
freshly chopped coriander leaves

1. Heat the oil and butter in a large saucepan, then add the onions and potatoes. Cook for 2–3 minutes, then add the cumin and coriander. Stir and cook for a further minute.

2. Peel the butternut squash and remove the seeds. Chop the flesh into chunks and add to the saucepan. Cook for 3–4 minutes, stirring well to coat in the butter and oil.

3. Add sufficient water to just cover (about 900 ml/1½ pints), bring to the boil, then reduce the heat and simmer, covered, for about 20–25 minutes.

4. Add the spinach and cook for a further 5 minutes, stirring well.

5. Add salt and pepper to taste, then purée (I like to use a hand-held blender; a food processor will do). Check the seasoning, then ladle into a warmed soup tureen and garnish with a dollop of Greek yoghurt and a sprinkling of coriander leaves. Serve with freshly baked granary and nut bread.

Granary and Nut Bread

25 g/1 oz fresh yeast
1 tsp honey, warmed
350–400 ml/12–14 fl oz water, warmed until tepid
500 g/1 lb strong white flour
250 g/8 oz granary flour
1½ tsp salt
50 g/2 oz butter, melted
50 g/2 oz hazelnuts, roughly chopped
40 g/1½ oz pine nut kernels
2 tsp hazelnut oil

1. Mix the yeast with the honey and about a quarter of the water, stir well and leave for about 5–10 minutes.

2. Mix together the white and granary flours, with the salt in a large bowl. Add the melted butter, the yeast mixture and enough of the remaining water to make a stiff dough.

3. Turn the dough on to a floured board and knead for about 10 minutes until smooth.

4. Place in a lightly oiled bowl, cover with clingfilm and leave in a warm place (such as an airing cupboard) for about 1 hour, or until the mixture has doubled in size.

5. Knock back the dough (with your fists), then knead in the hazelnuts and pine nut kernels. Divide the dough into two and roll these into ovals

(about 30 cm/12 inches long). Try to ensure there are no nuts poking out, or they will burn.

6. Brush with the hazelnut oil and leave to rise again, for 30–45 minutes.

7. Preheat the oven to Gas 7/220°C/425°F.

8. Bake the loaves for about 20 minutes, or until they sound hollow when the bottom is tapped.

THE SOUP CAN BE FROZEN, ALTHOUGH THE COLOUR MAY BE DULLER; THE BREAD FREEZES SUCCESSFULLY

Venison with Mushrooms and Polenta

1 whole venison fillet (about 500 g/1 lb)
2 tbsp extra virgin olive oil
2–3 tsp black peppercorns, coarsely ground in a
    pestle and mortar
$\frac{1}{2}$ tbsp Worcestershire sauce

FOR THE MUSHROOMS

50 g/2 oz unsalted butter
1 small onion, peeled, finely chopped
2–3 garlic cloves, peeled, crushed
250 g/8 oz ceps (porcini) or shiitake mushrooms,
    wiped, finely chopped
250 g/8 oz flat cap or button mushrooms, wiped
    finely chopped
15 g/$\frac{1}{2}$ oz plain flour
2 tbsp Madeira
150 ml/$\frac{1}{4}$ pint double cream
1–2 tbsp truffle oil
salt, pepper
(minced black truffle, optional)

FOR THE POLENTA

175 g/6 oz polenta
$\frac{1}{2}$ tsp salt
900 ml/1$\frac{1}{2}$ pints cold water
25 g/1 oz butter, melted

1. For the venison, brush the fillet with half the oil, then press the crushed
   black pepper all over. Cover and leave for a couple of hours.

2. Preheat the oven to Gas7/220°C/425°F. Heat the remaining oil with the Worcestershire sauce in a large frying pan until very hot. Brown the venison all over until sealed (this should take no more than 5 minutes). Transfer to an ovenproof dish, pouring any remaining oil and peppercorns from the frying pan over the venison, and place in the middle of the preheated oven, uncovered, for a maximum of 15 minutes. Then remove the meat to a carving board and wrap in double foil. Leave to rest for at least 10 minutes before cutting into slices.

3. For the mushrooms, heat the butter in a saucepan and fry the onion and garlic gently for about 5 minutes. Add the mushrooms and cook, covered, for about 10 minutes. Increase the heat, sprinkle in the flour, stir well then add the Madeira and cream. Bring to the boil, then reduce the heat and cook for another couple of minutes. Season to taste with salt and pepper, then remove from the heat. Stir in half the truffle oil.

4. Place the polenta, water and salt in a large saucepan and bring slowly to the boil. Stirring all the time, simmer for 5–10 minutes if you are using pre-cooked polenta, or 40 minutes for the traditional method. Taste for seasoning and stir in the butter.

5. To serve, place slices of the venison on to warmed plates, spoon some polenta alongside and some of the mushroom sauce. Drizzle a tiny amount of truffle oil (or sprinkle minced truffle) over the mushroom sauce and serve at once.

NONE OF THE MAIN COURSE SHOULD BE FROZEN

SEA BASS WITH RED PEPPER AND BASIL SAUCE

PLUMS IN SLOE GIN

Plums in Sloe Gin

500 g/1 lb ripe plums (such as Victoria plums)
50 g/2 oz light brown muscovado sugar
a dash of pure vanilla essence
4 tbsp sloe gin

TO SERVE

clotted cream

1. Preheat the oven to Gas 6/200°C/400°F.

2. Halve and stone the plums, then place them in an ovenproof dish.

3. Sprinkle the plums with the sugar and vanilla essence, then pour over the sloe gin.

4. Cover and bake in the preheated oven for about 25–30 minutes. Cool them and eat either at room temperature or barely warm. Serve with some thick clotted cream.

THE PLUMS DO NOT FREEZE WELL

Prior to his appointment as head chef at The Lygon Arms, Broadway, CLIVE HOWE worked at The Dorchester under Anton Mosimann. The emphasis in his restaurant is on using the best of British produce, sometimes cooked to an old English recipe (one of his hobbies is collecting old cookery books). His inspirational cooking style takes full advantages of local produce, particularly from the nearby Vale of Evesham. Here is one of Clive's recipes for venison, cooked with a beetroot and onion sauce.

Grilled Venison Steak with a Beetroot and Onion Sauce

4 × 150 g/5 oz venison steaks (trimmed, marinated
   in oil with herbs, shallots and garlic)
25 g/1 oz dried beetroot
100 g/3½ oz onion rings, floured
100 ml/3½ fl oz venison jus
100 g/3½ oz beetroot, grated and braised with red
   wine, redcurrant jelly and cinnamon
50 g/2 oz onions, sliced
50 ml/1½ fl oz port
25 g/1 oz chopped parsley and tarragon
sprigs of parsley and tarragon
25 g/1 oz butter
1 tbsp oil
seasoning

1. Oil the venison steaks, season, then char-grill them for 15 minutes, leaving them medium-rare.

2. Place the onion in a saucepan with the butter and sweat until soft and golden brown.

3. Add the braised beetroot, port and venison jus and reduce until you have a thick consistency.

4. Add the tarragon and parsley and season to taste.

5. In hot oil, deep-fry the onion rings and the dried beetroot, then drain on some kitchen paper.

6. Season and place around the edges of 4 warmed plates.

7. Pour a little of the sauce in the middle of each plate.

8. Cut the venison in half and place on the 4 plates.

9. Garnish with the parsley and tarragon sprigs.

Menu

Butter-bean and Herb Salad
Olive Oil Bread

Sea Bass with Red Pepper & Basil Sauce
Spinach with Sorrel

Strawberry and Cream Cheese
Ice-Cream

Three

As you see, this menu makes full use of summer produce. A salad of butter-beans with fresh garden herbs is followed by sea bass, which is common in English waters in midsummer. The fish is accompanied by a red pepper sauce, which is spiked with basil, my favourite summer herb. To follow, local strawberries – which taste infinitely better than foreign imports throughout the rest of the year – are in abundance; I make them into a wickedly rich ice-cream.

Dried butter-beans are often used in traditional British cooking, in soups, with casseroles or roasts. It is important not to salt the water you cook the butter-beans in, as this toughens their outer skins. I have used them in a fresh salad with tomatoes and herbs – parsley, thyme and, predominantly, marjoram. The latter tastes sweet and very aromatic. It is often used to flavour meat loaves, sausages and pizzas. Marjoram belongs to the same genus as oregano, but tastes less pungent and hot. Wild marjoram is common all over Britain, flowering from July to October. The flowers, which are white or pink, add an appropriate garnish to the salad, as they taste mildly spicy. I like to accompany the salad with an Italian-inspired olive oil bread, made with Italian flour.

Unless you live near the south coast, where sea bass tend to migrate in colder weather, it can be difficult to obtain this fish in the late winter months. You may be offered imported sea bass, but try to be patient and wait until the fish starts migrating northwards to other English waters – it is superior to the imported fish. The waters around Devon and Cornwall are best for this handsome silver fish, with its firm white flesh. It is delicious baked whole, with flavourings such as fennel, sorrel or ginger. It also lends itself to grilling, when cut into fillets. I like to rub the fillets well with olive oil and insert some basil into slits, to give added flavour. The chilli-flavoured oil I use with the red peppers is not essential, but it does add an edge to the finished sauce. A couple of shakes of Tabasco would make a reasonable substitute. I would continue to serve the warm Italian bread with this course, as well as a dish of lightly cooked spinach and sorrel. Sorrel grows wild throughout Britain and is used with many fish recipes, particularly salmon. Its sharp, citrus-flavoured acidity is also good to cut through fatty meats such as duck or pork. When adding sorrel to soups, it should be added at the very end and not allowed to boil, or its natural vivid green colour will turn a rusty brown.

The arrival of the strawberry season means the beginning of true summer. British strawberries always taste softer and sweeter than the imported varieties. I like nothing better than to spend a warm June afternoon at a Pick-Your-Own farm, cramming as many berries as possible into baskets, to make fresh strawberry jam. The children usually end up eating far too many and cannot face them again for tea with cream or – my favourite – crème fraîche. Gooseberries or redcurrants (with their higher level of pectin) ensure a good set when mixed into your strawberry jam. Actually, I am rather partial to runny strawberry jam, but it does mean it will not keep so well. Balsamic vinegar enhances the natural sweetness of the berries in this ice-cream, which is reminiscent of luscious strawberry cheesecake.

ADVANCE PREPARATION

The salad can be made the day before and refrigerated, but must be brought to room temperature for at least an hour. The red pepper sauce can be cooked a couple of hours in advance and reheated very gently; the fish and spinach need last-minute cooking. The ice-cream is better eaten on the day it is made.

WINE SUGGESTIONS

The big, fruity flavour of a Chardonnay wine is called for with the sea bass, and it can be served with the salad too. According to pocket or taste, either serve a Meursault from Burgundy, or Cooks Hawkes Bay Chardonnay from New Zealand. Stay with the Chardonnay for the pudding, if you wish, or serve a sweet Sauternes.

Butter-bean and Herb Salad

250 g/8 oz dried butter-beans, soaked overnight
1 bay leaf
4 tbsp extra virgin olive oil
1 tbsp sherry vinegar
1 spring onion, finely chopped
2 garlic cloves, peeled, crushed
1 tbsp freshly chopped marjoram
$\frac{1}{2}$ tbsp freshly chopped parsley
$\frac{1}{2}$ tbsp freshly chopped thyme leaves
salt, pepper
2 large tomatoes, peeled, chopped

TO SERVE

extra virgin olive oil
black olives, optional

1. Place the beans in a large saucepan of fresh water. Add the bay leaf, bring to the boil and simmer, covered, for about 2 hours, until the beans are tender.

2. Mix all the remaining ingredients, except the tomatoes, in a food processor, seasoning to taste with salt and pepper. Drain the beans and mix with the dressing while still warm. Let the mixture cool, then carefully stir in the tomatoes.

3. To serve, pour into a salad bowl (you can line this with lettuce leaves, if you like), and drizzle over a little olive oil and garnish with some black olives, if your guests like them.

Olive Oil Bread

25 g/1 oz fresh yeast
a pinch of sugar
300–350 ml/10–12 fl oz water, warmed to tepid
500 g/1 lb OO flour or strong white flour
1 tsp salt
2 tbsp olive oil

TO FINISH

coarse seas salt
olive oil, for brushing

1. Dissolve the yeast, with the sugar, in a quarter of the water and leave for 5–10 minutes, until frothy.

2. Sift the flour and salt into a large bowl. Add the yeast mixture with the olive oil and enough of the water to bind to the soft dough. Knead for about 10 minutes until smooth, then place in an oiled bowl, cover with clingfilm and leave in a warm place for about an hour.

3. Knock back the dough, then flatten and place on an oiled baking tray (ease out the dough to an oval shape). Press your knuckles all over the dough, to make dimples, then sprinkle over some coarsely ground sea salt. Brush liberally with olive oil, then return the dough to the warm place for a further 20–30 minutes, until risen again. Preheat the oven to Gas 8/230°C/450°F.

4. Bake the bread for about 20 minutes, until puffy and golden brown. Brush with some more olive oil and serve warm, in wedges.

THE SALAD CANNOT BE FROZEN; THE BREAD FREEZES WELL

Sea Bass with Red Pepper and Basil Sauce

4 fillets of sea bass (about 175 g/6 oz each)
olive oil for brushing
8 large basil leaves
salt, freshly ground pepper

RED PEPPER AND BASIL SAUCE

1 tbsp olive oil
1 tsp chilli-flavoured oil
1 garlic clove, peeled, crushed
2 shallots, peeled, finely chopped
2 red peppers, halved, seeded, chopped
12 large basil leaves
400 ml/14 oz fish stock
salt, pepper

TO SERVE

fresh basil sprigs

1. Make sure the sea bass is well scaled, then brush it all over with olive oil. Slash the skin of each fillet twice and insert basil leaves in each. Season with salt and pepper, cover with oiled clingfilm and leave for an hour.

2. For the sauce, heat the oils in a saucepan, add the garlic and shallots and gently fry for about 5 minutes. Add the red peppers and basil, then add the fish stock, bring to the boil, then reduce the heat and simmer, uncovered, for about 20 minutes. Transfer to a food processor and purée, then pass through a sieve. Add salt and pepper to taste, then keep the sauce warm while you cook the fish.

3. Heat the grill to high, then place the fillets, skin side down, under the grill to cook for about 5–6 minutes altogether, turning after about 3 minutes so the skin becomes crisp and brown. (The timing depends on the thickness of the fillets, so check after 5 minutes to see if it is cooked.)

4. Transfer the fish to warmed serving plates, surround with some of the sauce and decorate with a sprig of basil. Offer the spinach in a separate dish.

Spinach with Sorrel

625 g/1¼ lb young spinach leaves,
125 g/4 oz young sorrel leaves,
1 tbsp extra virgin olive oil
15 g/½ oz unsalted butter
2 garlic cloves, peeled, crushed
salt, freshly ground black pepper

1. Pick over the spinach and sorrel and remove any coarse stalks. Wash the leaves well.

2. Heat the oil and butter in a saucepan, then add the garlic. Fry gently for 2–3 minutes, then add the spinach and sorrel, with just the water clinging to their leaves after washing.

3. Sauté briefly, for no more than 2–3 minutes, then season well, to taste, and serve at once, in a warmed dish.

NONE OF THE MAIN COURSE SHOULD BE FROZEN

Strawberry and Cream Cheese Ice-Cream

750 g/1½ lb strawberries, hulled, sliced
75 g/3 oz sugar
2 tbsp balsamic vinegar
300 g/10 oz cream cheese
2 tbsp fromage frais
300 ml/10 fl oz double cream
1 tbsp icing sugar

TO SERVE

strawberries, to garnish

1. In a bowl, toss the strawberries with the sugar and balsamic vinegar. Stirring occasionally, leave for about an hour.

2. Pour the contents of the bowl into a liquidiser and purée, or blend in a food processor; then press through a fine sieve.

3. Beat the cream cheese with the fromage frais, until soft.

4. Add the strawberry purée to the cream cheese mixture and combine well, until smooth.

5. Whip the cream with the icing sugar until floppy, then fold into the strawberry mixture until well mixed. (Use a balloon whisk if necessary.)

6. Pour into an ice-cream machine and churn until frozen (my machine takes only 20 minutes) or place in a container in the freezer and, beating every half hour, freeze until solid.

7. Remove from the freezer 20–25 minutes before serving, in spoonfuls, decorated with some fresh strawberries.

THE ICE-CREAM SHOULD NOT BE FROZEN FOR
LONGER THAN 2–3 WEEKS

(Helmut Claus)

Since RICK STEIN and his wife Jill opened The Seafood Restaurant in Cornwall nearly 20 years ago, it has attracted regular customers from not only all over England, but also from the USA, Japan and Australia. Highly recommended in all restaurant and hotel guides, it is Rick's skilful preparation of the freshest ingredients and his accomplished and clever combinations of flavours which lure guests to his fish restaurant overlooking the harbour in Padstow. It is apposite that Rick's recipe uses sea bass, which is plentiful in the waters around Cornwall.

Roast Sea Bass with Red Cabbage and Rosti Potatoes

FOR THE RED CABBAGE

300 g/10 oz red cabbage
125 g/4 oz onion, diced
150 ml/5 fl oz red wine
2 tbsp wine vinegar
1 tbsp salt
1 tbsp sugar
150 ml/5 fl oz fish (or chicken) stock
50 g/2 oz butter

1. Preheat the oven to Gas 6/200°C/400°F. Remove the outer leaves of the cabbage and cut out the thickest of the white core. Slice the cabbage as thinly as possible, then turn the slices round and cut them into the smallest possible pieces. Put all the red cabbage ingredients, except half the stock and all the butter, in an ovenproof dish and place in the oven with the lid on, for about one hour and 15 minutes. Check occasionally that the cabbage is not burning and turn the ingredients over with a spoon. (The cabbage may be cooked in advance.)

FOR THE ROSTI POTATOES

425 g/14 oz potatoes
25 g/1 oz smoked bacon (or pancetta), cut into
    thin strips
salt, pepper
clarified butter, to fry

2. Peel the potatoes and shred them on the largest grid of a cheese grater on
to a clean tea-towel. Gather the edges of the tea-towel and squeeze as
much moisture out of the potatoes as you can. (You don't need to rinse
them: you want to retain the starch, which binds them together.) Season
the potato with salt and pepper and add the bacon (pancetta). Divide
into 4 equal balls.

3. Pour plenty of clarified butter into a small (15 cm/6 inch) non-stick (or
well-tempered) frying pan. Add one of the balls of potato and bacon.
Flatten this out over the whole of the base of the pan with a fish slice and
fry over a medium heat for about 4 minutes. Work the fish slice under the
pancake, to free it, then turn it over and cook on the other side for 4
minutes. Towards the end of cooking, press the excess butter out of the
rosti on some kitchen paper and pour it off. Place the rosti on some
kitchen paper, to remove any greasiness. Do this with the other 3 balls.

FOR THE FISH

1 sea bass (weighing 1.5–2 kg/$3\frac{1}{2}$–$4\frac{1}{2}$ lb)
$\frac{1}{2}$ tsp salt
20 turns of the black peppermill
1 clove, grated finely
a little melted butter·

4. Increase your oven to its maximum temperature. Brush the bass inside
and out with melted butter and sprinkle inside and out with the salt,
pepper and clove. Place on a roasting tray in the very hot oven for about
30 minutes, basting regularly with the juices from the tray.

5. To serve, add the remaining stock to the red cabbage and bring to the boil, then stir in the butter. Place the fish on a large oval plate and pour over the juices from the pan. Serve the bass at the table, giving each person a rosti potato, a generous portion of the red cabbage with plenty of the liquid, and some sea bass with the skin.

Four

THERE ARE ROBUST FLAVOURS IN BOTH THE STARTER AND MAIN COURSES of this menu. They are followed by a tangy, creamy dream of a pudding. It is good old-fashioned bread and butter pudding with a difference. I use fresh lemon curd to spread on to the layers, which are not sliced white bread, but brioche. The result is a beautifully light texture and tangy citrus taste. It is preceded by a pasta starter with Brie and fennel, then beef with a crust of fresh tarragon, thyme and parsley – warming fare to appease hearty appetites.

For the starter, I recommend using freshly made pasta, but good quality dried will do. Instead of Brie, I often like to use a local cheese, Bonchester. It is made by John Curtis at Easter Weens farm, near Hawick, in the Scottish Borders. Made by traditional methods from Jersey cows' milk, Bonchester is very rich and creamy, reminiscent of the best Brie or Camembert. If Bonchester is unavailable, use a ripe, runny Brie *fermier*. Florence fennel, with its aniseed flavour, complements the cheese in this gutsy starter. Bronze fennel or the feathery fronds on top of fennel bulbs make a suitable garnish.

A deciding factor in your choice of beef is whether it has been well hung. Modern methods often mean that it is hardly hung at all, before being packaged under supermarket wrappers. Traditional methods mean that the meat is matured on the bone for about two weeks, for the true flavour to develop and for it to become tender. Properly hung beef should not have a bright red colour, but a rather darker hue; it should also appear slightly moist and be marbled with sufficient fat to prevent it drying out. The forerib of beef is ideal for roasting. It is not only much cheaper than sirloin; my butcher believes it is also tastier, which is proof enough for me!

The type of fresh herbs can be varied, but I would suggest the inclusion of tarragon, whose distinctive flavour enhances any roast meat. It should be added with caution, tasting as you mix, for its taste is powerful enough to completely dominate other flavours. Dried tarragon usually tastes more like hay than a herb, so if you have a surplus of fresh, you can quickly freeze

Menu

Pasta with Brie and Fennel

Beef with Herb Crust
Roast Parsnips • Glazed Shallots

Lemon Curd Bread & Butter Pudding

it, or make your own tarragon vinegar. To do this, fill a bottle with fresh tarragon, cover with white wine vinegar, seal and leave for about six weeks. Strain into a clean bottle, and push in a fresh sprig of tarragon.

I think roast parsnips and glazed shallots are good with the roast beef. But other root vegetables, such as celeriac or baby beetroot would also roast very well alongside the meat.

There are so many variations on the traditionally British bread and butter pudding. Sometimes they are layered with apricot jam or sultanas, sometimes they are made with white bread, sometimes with wholemeal bread rolls. I have a friend, Fiona, who always makes a bread and butter pudding for the family with layers of fresh lemon curd. It is quite delicious. Home-made lemon curd is nothing like the garish yellow shop-bought variety, and does not take long to make. It lasts for up to six weeks in the fridge. In my recipe, I have used brioche instead of white or brown bread, as I like the light texture. Being a sweet, enriched dough, the amount of sugar normally used is reduced. The classical round brioche, which is easiest to buy, is ideal for the pudding, as it fits perfectly into a round 1.2 litre/2 pint baking or soufflé dish.

ADVANCE PREPARATION

The starter cannot be cooked in advance. The beef can be trimmed and the crust prepared in advance, but should be cooked just in time for serving. The lemon curd pudding is better freshly baked, though it does taste good cold too.

WINE SUGGESTIONS

The beef requires a fine Bordeaux, or Burgundy, which can be served at the start with the pasta and Brie. A 10-year-old Barsac will be an elegant finish to a meal full of classic ingredients.

49

Pasta with Brie and Fennel

$\frac{1}{2}$ tbsp olive oil
2 garlic cloves, peeled, crushed
1 large fennel bulb (about 300 g/10oz), coarse
    outer leaves removed
125 ml/4 fl oz double cream
125 g/4 oz Brie or Bonchester, rind removed,
    chopped
salt, pepper
175–200 g/6–7 oz dried tagliatelle (if using fresh,
    use recipe in Chapter Eight)

TO SERVE

2–3 rashers of smoked back bacon, grilled until
    crisp
bronze fennel or fennel fronds

1. Heat the olive oil in a saucepan and add the garlic. Finely slice the fennel and add to the pan. Stir, cover with a lid and cook over a low heat for about 10 minutes, until the vegetables are just softened.

2. Add the cream, bring to the boil, then reduce the heat to very low and add the cheese. Stir well and cook gently, until the cheese is melted, stirring all the time.

3. Season to taste with salt and plenty of pepper.

4. Cook the pasta until it is just tender, then drain well and divide it between 4 warmed bowls. Spoon the fennel and cheese mixture on top of the pasta and crumble over the cripsy bacon. Garnish with bronze fennel or fennel fronds. Eat at once.

THE STARTER CANNOT BE FROZEN

Beef with Herb Crust

SERVES 8

2–2.25 kg/4½–5 lb forerib or sirloin of beef (on the
   bone), trimmed
15 g/½ oz butter
½ tbsp olive oil

FOR THE CRUST

65 g/2½ oz fresh breadcrumbs
1 tbsp freshly chopped thyme
1 tbsp freshly chopped tarragon
2 tbsp freshly chopped parsley
1 tsp horseradish relish
2 garlic cloves, peeled, crushed
15 g/½ oz melted butter
salt, pepper
1 large egg white, whisked until stiff

FOR THE SAUCE

300 ml/10 fl oz well-flavoured beef stock
150 ml/5 fl oz full-bodied red wine
15 g/½ oz butter, diced
salt, freshly ground pepper

1. Preheat the oven to Gas 7/220°C/425°F.

2. Heat the butter and oil in a roasting tin until very hot. Place the beef in
   the tin and turn it all over, to coat with the hot fat. Roast in the oven for
   15 minutes, then remove the meat from the tin to a board, and reduce
   the heat to Gas 5/190°C/375°F.

3. For the crust, combine all the ingredients except the egg white (I use a food processor, though a bowl will do). Add salt and pepper, then fold in the egg white.

4. Carefully press the crust mixture over the top (and ends) of the beef, so it is covered with a very thin crust. Return the beef carefully to the roasting tin, and place in the oven to roast for 15 minutes per 500 g/1 lb for rare meat; add on an extra 15 minutes for medium-rare or 30 for medium. The crust should be golden brown. (Cover it with foil if it becomes too brown, towards the end of cooking.)

5. Remove to a carving board, loosely cover with foil and rest for 15 minutes.

6. Meanwhile, make the sauce. Skim off most of the fat from the roasting tin, then, placing over a direct heat, deglaze the pan with the red wine (stirring to scrape up all the flavours from the tin), then add the stock and reduce, over a high heat, until slightly syrupy. Lower the heat slightly, then add the butter, whisking after each piece is put in, then season to taste with salt and pepper. Strain the sauce and serve with the beef. (This is a rather thin sauce; if you prefer it thicker, add $\frac{1}{2}$ tsp plain flour, as you deglaze, then add the wine.)

7. Carve the beef into slices and serve on warmed plates, with the sauce.

Roast Parsnips

625–750 g/1¼–1½ lb thick parsnips, peeled
25 g/1 oz butter
2 tbsp olive oil

1. Preheat the oven to Gas 5/190°C/375°F.

2. Halve and then quarter the parsnips lengthways. Remove any woody cores.

3. Parboil the parsnips in boiling salted water for 3 minutes, then drain very well (I usually cover them with a tea-towel to absorb any excess moisture).

4. Heat the butter and oil in a baking tin in the oven for a couple of minutes, until it is hot. Then toss in the parsnips, basting well and roast them (under the beef) for about 50 minutes, or until golden brown. Baste a couple of times with the fat. Drain on kitchen paper, before serving.

Glazed Shallots

375 g/12 oz shallots, peeled, left whole
15 g/½ butter
½ tsp sugar
salt

1. Place the shallots in a saucepan with barely enough water to cover. Add the butter, sugar and a good pinch of salt. Bring to the boil, cover and reduce the heat. Simmer for about 15 minutes, until the shallots are just tender.

2. Remove the lid, increase the heat and cook for a further 15 minutes or so, until the shallots are golden brown and shiny all over. It is important to vigorously shake the pan (do not stir, or you will break up the shallots) every minute.

NONE OF THE MAIN COURSE CAN BE FROZEN

Lemon Curd Bread and Butter Pudding

FOR THE LEMON CURD

3 eggs, beaten and sieved
the grated zest of 3 large lemons (preferably
    unwaxed)
175 ml/6 fl oz freshly squeezed lemon juice
125 g/4 oz unsalted butter, in pieces
250 g/8 oz granulated sugar

FOR THE PUDDING

1 round brioche (about 300–375 g/10–12oz)
50 g/2 oz unsalted butter, softened
4 tbsp lemon curd
2 eggs plus 1 egg yolk, beaten
50 g/2 oz caster sugar
300 ml/10 fl oz milk
150 ml/5 fl oz double cream

1. For the lemon curd, mix the eggs with the lemon zest and juice in a bowl.
   Add the butter and sugar and mix well. Place in the top of a double
   boiler, or in a bowl over a pan of simmering water. Heat gently, stirring
   or whisking constantly, until the sugar dissolves and the mixture
   thickens. This takes about 20 minutes. Cool, then use as required.

2. Cut the brioche into 4 or 5 thin slices, lengthwise. Spread the slices with
   the butter and then the lemon curd.

3. Preheat the oven to Gas 3/160°C/325°F. Butter a round 1.2 litre/2 pint
   ovenproof or soufflé dish. Place the slices carefully in the dish, one on top
   of the other.

4. Whisk together the eggs, egg yolk, sugar, milk and cream. Strain this over the brioche in the dish. Let it soak in for about 30 minutes, at room temperature.

5. Place the dish in a roasting pan half-filled with hot water, and bake in the preheated oven for about 40–45 minutes, or until the custard is set round the edges and slightly wobbly in the very centre.

6. Leave to cool for a few minutes, then serve, with or without pouring cream.

NONE OF THE PUDDING SHOULD BE FROZEN

ANTHONY TOBIN became head chef at South Lodge, West Sussex, after five years spent working under Nico Ladenis in London. His recipes are simple in concept and made only with the finest ingredients. In the restaurant, there is an emphasis on British food: for example, traditional puddings feature strongly on his menu. Anthony's cooking incorporates wonderful combinations of flavours, and, fired by his youthful enthusiasm, he creates memorable dishes, such as his fresh ravioli of langoustine.

Fresh Ravioli of Langoustine with Sweet Peppers and its own Vinaigrette

FOR THE PASTA

2 whole eggs plus 3 yolks
250 g/8 oz flour
a pinch of salt
1 tsp olive oil

1. Put the eggs, salt and oil into a blender and switch on. Slowly add the flour and process until a loose ball of dough is formed. Knead on a smooth surface until the dough is smooth, then cut into 4, wrap in clingfilm and rest for 15 minutes.

FOR THE VINAIGRETTE

12 langoustine heads and shells (after you have removed the flesh for the filling)
trimmings from 1 red, 1 green, 1 yellow pepper (once you have prepared the garnish)
2 shallots, chopped
1 small carrot, 1 celery stick, 1 small leek, finely diced

2 sprigs each of tarragon and thyme
1 bay leaf
1 tbsp tomato purée
4 peppercorns
$\frac{1}{4}$ cup white wine vinegar
$\frac{1}{2}$ cup white wine
1 cup olive oil

2. Place the langoustines, peppers, shallots, carrots, celery, leeks and herbs in a pan and sweat for 5 minutes. Then add the tomato purée and cook for a further 5 minutes. Add all the liquid and bring to the boil. Place in a low oven for 1 hour, then remove, pass through a fine sieve and allow to cool.

FOR THE FILLING

75 g/3 oz salmon trimmings or tail
12 langoustines (heads off and peeled, for use in
   the vinaigrette)
4 tbsp double cream
salt, pepper

3. Place the salmon trimmings in a processor and whizz to a smooth paste, then add the cream and seasoning and whizz for a further 5 seconds. Chop up the langoustines and add to the salmon mixture. Place in a bowl and refrigerate.

FOR THE RAVIOLI

4. Roll the pasta in a pasta machine until it is at No. 2 thickness. Then place 1 tsp of the filling at 5 cm/2in intervals all the way along the centre. Brush around the edges with egg wash and fold over.

5. Press down firmly and cut half way between each mound with a fluted cutter. Allow 5 per person.

6. To cook, place the ravioli into salted, boiling water for 2 minutes, then drain well.

FOR THE GARNISH

    1 red, 1 yellow, 1 green pepper, peeled and cut
      into dice or ribbons.
    2 tomatoes, skinned, deseeded, coarsely chopped
    1 tbsp chopped chives

7. To serve, warm the garnish through in the vinaigrette, in a small saucepan.

8. Place the freshly cooked ravioli around a warmed plate, curved side facing out. Spoon the garnish into the centre and pour the vinaigrette over the ravioli.

Menu

Jerusalem Artichoke and
Smoked Haddock Soup

Cod with Rosemary
Ratatouille Mounds

Dark Treacle Ice-Cream
with Lemon Shortbread

Five

THERE ARE TWISTS OF CLASSICAL DISHES IN THIS MENU. THE SOUP IS A variation of Cullen Skink, a traditional soup from the north east coast of Scotland which uses Finnan haddock or smoked haddock fillets and potatoes. I have used Jerusalem artichokes instead of potatoes, and added a drizzle of fruity olive oil at the end. The cod is cooked with aromatic rosemary in a roasting bag in the oven. These bags are more often used for joints of meat, but are, in fact, perfect for fish as they remove the danger of the delicate flesh drying out. The dessert uses the two essentials ingredients for treacle tart: treacle and fresh lemon zest. The two combine beautifully in an ice-cream with buttery shortbread.

For the soup, undyed smoked haddock fillets are poached, then returned to the pan once the vegetables have been cooked. As Finnan haddock (or smoked haddock fillet) is cold smoked (unlike another smoked haddock, the Arbroath smokie, which is hot smoked and therefore requires no further cooking), the poaching not only flavours the liquid for the soup, it also cooks the fish. If possible, try to buy whole Finnan haddock, as its flavour is superior.

Jerusalem artichokes are favourite winter vegetables of mine, though they can be a nuisance to peel, with their knobbly exterior. Their sweet, delicate flavour is delicious in soups, purées and gratins. Once they have been peeled, you must plunge them immediately into the cooking liquid, or they will discolour. If there is to be any time lapse, put them in a bowl of water with a few drops of lemon juice.

For the cod, ask your fishmonger to give you a middle-cut piece, without either bones or skin. It is cooked with some very finely sliced leek and carrot, Noilly Prat (although you could use a white wine instead) and sprigs of fresh rosemary. Although rosemary is more often used with lamb, it is also good with chicken, pork, some fish and can be added to scones, breads and fruit salads. With cod, the most commonly used round white fish from British shores, it enhances the savoury flavour with its pungency. When you are opening up the roasting bags, to drain off the juices for the sauce, be careful not to burn yourself, as the cod is cooked in a very hot oven. The use of roasting bags here is not a form of *en papillote*, where the pleasure of opening the bag is savoured by guests at the table; apart from the fact that plastic roasting bags are not the most aesthetically pleasing vision, you need the juices for your buttery sauce. You can serve tiny steamed potatoes with the fish, if you like, as well as the ratatouille mounds. These are layers of the basic ratatouille components – aubergines, courgettes and tomatoes – cooked in ramekins and inverted on to the serving plate. They look good and have a surprise element of a whole basil leaf nestling within their depths.

The dark treacle ice-cream is made with black treacle, not golden syrup – which is, incongruously, used in treacle tarts. Apart from its culinary use in gingerbreads, toffee and rich fruit cakes, it has other uses at Hallowe'en, in Scotland. As children, we used to stand, hands behind our backs, and attempt to take bites of large scones plastered with black treacle, which were suspended by string from the washing line above. Luckily this was always followed by 'dooking' for apples which washed away most of the sticky black treacle from our faces! Surprisingly, these memories have not changed my feelings for treacle and I do still rather enjoy its strong lingering flavour. The ice-cream has a lovely deep brown colour and rich creamy texture. The lemon biscuits are short, buttery and tangy. They keep well in an airtight tin, and are just the thing with a cup of morning coffee.

ADVANCE PREPARATION

The soup can be prepared up to the end of stage 3, then reheated. The bags of cod can be prepared about half an hour in advance, but should be cooked at the last minute. The treacle ice-cream and lemon biscuits are best made fresh on the day.

WINE SUGGESTIONS

A full-bodied Chardonnay will go well with the first two dishes: a Chablis, if you do not want an over-pronounced oaky taste, Wolf Blass Chardonnay if you do. The Dark Treacle Ice-Cream is not as sweet as you might think: serve a Malmsey Madeira which has a pronounced flavour, without being too sweet.

Jerusalem Artichoke and Smoked Haddock Soup

500 g/1 lb smoked haddock fillets
600 ml/1 pint water
1 large onion, peeled, finely chopped
1 kg/2 lb Jerusalem artichokes, peeled, cut into
    chunks
freshly ground pepper

TO SERVE

extra virgin olive oil, to drizzle

1. Place the haddock in the water in a large saucepan. Bring to the boil, then simmer, covered, for about 5–6 minutes, until the fish is just cooked. Remove the fish with a slotted spoon and set aside.

2. Add the onions and Jerusalem artichokes to the pan, with a good grinding of pepper. Cover and cook over a moderate heat for about 15 minutes, or until the vegetables are tender.

3. Remove from the heat, add about two-thirds of the reserved fish and blend (I like to use a hand-held blender) until smooth.

4. Reheat gently, until the soup is piping hot, season to taste, then ladle into warmed soup bowls. Divide the remaining fish into four and flake it over the soup. Finish with a drizzle of olive oil.

THE SOUP CAN BE FROZEN UP TO THE END OF STAGE 3

Cod with Rosemary

4 × 200 g/7 oz middle-cut pieces of boneless cod
    fillet
1 leek, cleaned
2 carrots, peeled
4 sprigs of fresh rosemary (about 6 cm/2½ inches
    long)
125 ml/4 fl oz Noilly Prat
150 ml/5 fl oz fish stock
salt, pepper
100 g/3½ oz cold unsalted butter, cubed
(You will need 4 roasting bags)

1. Preheat the oven to Gas 8/230C/450F.

2. Remove the fish from the fridge at least half an hour before using. Cut the carrots and leeks into juliennes (very fine matchstick shapes) and drop them into a pan of boiling salted water for 1–2 minutes. Drain well.

3. Place the 4 oven bags on a baking tray and open them up. Divide the vegetables between them. Place a sprig of rosemary on each, then the cod fillet on top. Season with salt and pepper. Mix the Noilly Prat and fish stock together in a jug and divide it between the 4 bags.

4. Tightly seal the bags (near the top, so there is plenty room inside the bags), cut a tiny slit at the top of each bag, and place the baking tray in the middle of the oven. Cook for about 10 minutes, or until the liquid starts to bubble.

5. Remove from the oven and carefully snip a very small hole in the bottom of each bag (with very sharp scissors). Carefully drain all the juices out, into a small clean saucepan. Using a large fish-slice, carefully slide out the fish and vegetables on to warmed plates. (To keep the plates warm, place them in the oven once you have switched off the heat, and leave the door open.)

COD WITH ROSEMARY

LEMON CURD BREAD AND BUTTER PUDDING

6. Bring the juices in the saucepan to the boil and reduce them to half. Then add the butter, a little at a time, whisking madly, until you have a sauce-like consistency. Season to taste and pour over the fish.

Ratatouille Mounds

1 aubergine, wiped
2 courgettes, wiped
2 tomatoes
2 tbsp olive oil
2 garlic cloves, peeled, crushed
4 large basil leaves
salt, pepper
4 tsp passata (thick sieved tomatoes)

1. Slice the aubergine into very thin rounds, about 3 mm/$\frac{1}{8}$ inch. Sprinkle with salt and leave for 30 minutes.

2. Wipe or wash the salt off, and pat dry with kitchen paper.

3. Slice the courgettes and tomatoes, to the same thinness.

4. Heat the oil and gently fry the garlic for a minute, then add the aubergine and courgette and fry for 2–3 minutes, until browned. (You will probably have to do this in 2 batches.)

5. Generously oil 4 ramekins (8 cm/3 inches). Preheat the oven to Gas 6/ 200°C/400°F.

6. Layer the ramekins with aubergines, then tomato, then courgette, seasoning as you go. Then add a whole basil leaf, and continue filling the ramekin to the top, finishing with an aubergine. Press down firmly, using the back of a spoon. Spoon 1 tsp passata over each, press down again and bake them in the preheated oven for about 25 minutes, until the vegetables are tender.

7. Remove them from the oven, let them rest for 5 minutes, then invert on to warmed plates. (You can cook these in advance, then reheat for 5 minutes in the very hot oven below the cod.)

NONE OF THE MAIN COURSE CAN BE FROZEN

Dark Treacle Ice-Cream with Lemon Shortbread

FOR THE ICE-CREAM

150 ml/5 fl oz milk
150 ml/5 fl oz double cream
4 egg yolks (size 2)
2 rounded tbsp black treacle
a pinch of salt
150 ml/5 fl oz soured cream

FOR THE SHORTBREAD

125 g/4 oz unsalted butter, softened
65 g/2½ oz caster sugar
the grated zest of half a lemon
1 tsp freshly squeezed lemon juice
125 g/4 oz plain flour, sifted

1. For the ice-cream, place the milk and double cream in a saucepan over a low heat.

2. Beat the egg yolks with the treacle until it is creamy. Add the salt.

3. When the milk mixture has nearly reached boiling point, remove from the heat and strain into the treacle mixture, whisking constantly. Cover closely (so a skin cannot form) and allow to become quite cold.

4. Once it has cooled, stir in the soured cream and churn the mixture in an ice-cream machine until frozen (or freeze in a bowl and beat every half hour). It should be served straight from the freezer, as it does not have a completely solid consistency.

5. For the shortbread, preheat the oven to Gas 3/160°C/325°F. Cream the butter and sugar until light and fluffy. Add the lemon zest and juice and beat well. Gradually fold in the flour.

6. Using your hand, quickly combine the mixture (with a light touch) to a soft dough. Do not overwork the dough.

7. Roll out the dough as thinly as possible, then cut out with round pastry or biscuit-cutters. Place these on a buttered baking tray.

8. Bake the biscuits in the oven for about 15 minutes, or until they are a pale golden colour. Remove to a wire rack to cool.

THE BISCUITS FREEZE WELL

(Jacqueline Richardson Press and
PR Consultants)

The trademark of **GARY RHODES'** cooking is 'the best of British'. The popularity of traditional dishes, such as faggots, Lancashire hotpot and bread and butter pudding on his menu, is proof that good British cooking is alive and well. This resurgence owes much to talented young chefs such as Gary, who is now in charge of the kitchens at The Greenhouse, London. Previously, he had been head chef at The Castle, Taunton; he has worked for Brian Turner at The Capital in Knightsbridge, and he has cooked in other kitchens. Gary's delicious recipe for fillet of cod on mashed potato exemplifies his honest and simple approach to food.

Fillet of Cod on Mashed Potato with a Lentil and Mustard Sauce

$4 \times 175-250$ g/6–8 oz cod fillet
125 g/4 oz lentils
450 ml/$\frac{3}{4}$ pint chicken stock
25 g/1 oz each of chopped onion, celery and carrot
butter
a little flour
Meaux mustard
mashed potatoes (finished with cream, butter and
  nutmeg)

FOR THE FISH SAUCE

600 ml/1 pint fish stock
2 glasses white wine
1 shallot or $\frac{1}{4}$ onion, chopped
1 bay leaf
mushroom stalks
300 ml/$\frac{1}{2}$ pint double cream
salt, pepper

1. For the fish sauce, place the shallots, bayleaf and mushrooms in a pan with the white wine. Reduce until almost dry, then add the fish stock and reduce again by two-thirds. Add the cream and bring to the boil. Cook this very slowly, for about 20 minutes. When it is cooked, season with salt and pepper and strain through a sieve.

2. To braise the lentils, sweat the onion, carrot and celery in some butter until soft, then add the lentils. Add the stock, bring to the boil, then reduce to a simmer. Cover with greaseproof paper and a lid, then place in a moderate oven (Gas 4/180°C/350°F) until the lentils are tender.

3. For the fish, season the fillets with salt and pepper and lightly flour the presentation side. Heat a frying pan and add a few drops of oil. Place the cod in the oil and cook until golden brown. Turn the fish over in the pan and continue to cook for a few minutes.

4. Add some of the lentils to the sauce and flavour with the mustard.

5. Spoon the mashed potatoes on to 4 warmed plates and spoon the lentil sauce around. Sit the cod on top of the mashed potatoes and serve at once.

Menu

Pickled Herring in Seaweed
Rye Bread Rolls

Rack of Lamb with Mint Pesto
Mushroom and Potato Ramekins

Hazelnut and Chocolate
Fudge Tart

Six

E ARLY SUMMER IS A GOOD TIME TO COOK THIS MENU, AS HERRING ARE AT their best – they are at their plumpest and most flavoursome. New season's lamb is also still in its prime and, combined with local fresh mint, it makes a very tasty and rather splendid dish. The dessert, a hazelnut and chocolate fudge tart, is my idea of heaven – at any time of year!

I remember eating herring as a child – either rolled in oatmeal and fried, or soused in vinegar, with onion rings, and served cold. I always preferred the former, as vinegar can be overpowering for a young palate. Having then tried herring in various guises in Denmark and Finland, my enthusiasm has grown for this highly nutritious oily fish. Rolling the herring into rollmops was always a slippery business, although the end result was good. Here I have rolled the fish first in dried seaweed (having tried several, I find Nori is best); this not only adds an extra layer of colour, but makes the rolling precedure a lot easier. Nori (*Porphyra tenera*) is most commonly used for Sushi; it can also be toasted and crumbled over salads or vegetables. Another dried seaweed, Wakame (*Undaria pinnatifida*), needs to be soaked first, then toasted or fried, before crumbling over soups or salads. At The But 'n Ben in Auchmithie, near Arbroath, Margaret Horn, who has eaten seaweed regularly since childhood, collects it herself at low tide to serve in her restaurant. Margaret wraps tangles (*Laminaria digitata*) and dulse (*Rhodymenia palmata*) round North Sea haddock and poaches it. She also grills dulse until it is crispy and sprinkles it with vinegar, either as a garnish or to eat on its own; and she adds dulse to potato and leek soups for a taste of the sea (and a beautiful green colour). I serve rye bread rolls with the herring. Since rye flour has very little gluten, it should be mixed with wheat flour in all breadmaking. It is often used in sourdough bread 'starters' (which are left to 'sour' for a couple of days before mixing with other ingredients and baking), because of its distinctively rich yet sour taste.

The mint pesto to coat the lamb should be made with spearmint (the most common garden mint) or peppermint (the latter has a much stronger

71

flavour so less should be used) or any other smooth-leaved mint. Round-leaved mints such as apple mint or Bowles mint can also be used, as the 'woolly' texture of their leaves disappears on chopping. The lamb is accompanied by a creamy little mound of potatoes and mushrooms, which are also good as a vegetarian main course, perhaps with some grated cheese on top. I would serve a fresh salad of green leaves such as frisée or cos lettuce in a simple vinaigrette, to follow.

There is a hazelnut crust to the tart. Try to grind your own nuts – the flavour is so much better. Place the hazelnuts on a baking tray in a moderate oven (about Gas 4/150°C/350°F) and roast for about 15 minutes, until they are golden brown. Then place them in a kitchen towel and, after about 5 minutes, rub them with the towel to remove the skins. Grind the nuts in a food processor or coffee grinder (making sure there are no residual coffee aromas). The chocolate in the filling should have about 50–60 per cent cocoa solids; one with 70 per cent would be too bitter for the sweet, gooey, fudge-like filling. It is decadently rich, so small wedges should be proffered . . . at least to start with!

ADVANCE PREPARATION

The herrings should be cooked the day before and chilled, then brought to room temperature to serve. The mint pesto can be made in advance; surplus can be stored in a screw-top jar for about a month. The lamb and potato dishes should be freshly cooked. The tart is better on the day it is made.

WINE SUGGESTIONS

The vinegar in the Pickled Herring would destroy the taste of any wine. Try serving ice-cold Aquavit instead (but in small Schnapps glasses – it is strongly alcoholic). To follow, serve a Bulgarian Cabernet Sauvignon, Suhindol. If you wish to serve wine with the pudding, Quady Elysium California Black Muscat will complement the chocolate and hazelnut well.

Pickled Herring in Seaweed

6–8 fresh herring fillets, skinned (each about
   40–50 g/1½–2 oz)
3–4 tsp horseradish relish (or Wasabi paste)
salt, pepper
2 sheets Nori (edible seaweed)
1 medium onion, peeled, sliced finely
3–4 bay leaves
4 cloves
1 pinch mace
1 heaped tbsp black peppercorns
½ tsp allspice
125 ml/4 fl oz white wine vinegar
125 ml/4 fl oz distilled vinegar
125 ml/4 fl oz water
1 heaped tsp soft brown sugar

1. Sprinkle the flesh of the herring fillets with salt and pepper, then spread half a tsp of the horseradish relish over each. Cut the Nori sheets to the same width and length as the fillets, then lay the fish on the Nori and roll up tightly. Place half of the onions in an ovenproof dish, with the bay leaves, then lay the fish on top, packing them tightly together so they do not unroll. Top with the remaining onions.

2. In a saucepan, mix the remaining ingredients together and bring to the boil. Simmer, covered, for 10 minutes, then allow to cool for 20–30 minutes. Preheat the oven to Gas 4/180°C/350°F.

3. Pour the mixture from the saucepan over the herring, cover and place in the oven for 20–25 minutes.

4. Remove and leave to cool in the liquid for several hours (or overnight). Refrigerate, once cold.

5. To serve, bring the dish back to room temperature; then, with a slotted spoon, remove the fish and serve, either cut in half to reveal the two layers, or whole, garnished with a couple of the onion rings. Offer the warm rye bread rolls with unsalted butter.

Rye Bread Rolls

25 g/1 oz fresh yeast
350–400 ml/12–14 fl oz skimmed milk (or half
   milk, half water), warmed to tepid
2 tsp golden syrup
250 g/8 oz strong white flour
375 g/12 oz rye flour
2 tsp salt
40 g/1½ oz butter, melted and cooled slightly

TO FINISH

milk, to brush
1 tsp wheatgerm

1. Dissolve the yeast in half of the milk, with the syrup. Stir well and leave for 5 minutes.

2. Mix the two flours together with the salt in a large bowl. Add the yeast mixture, the butter and enough of the remaining milk to combine to a soft dough.

3. Knead for about 10 minutes, until smooth.

4. Place the dough in an oiled bowl, cover and place it somewhere warm for about an hour.

5. Knock back the dough, form into rolls and place on a buttered baking tray. Brush with a little milk and the wheatgerm. Return to the warm place for 30 minutes. Preheat the oven to Gas 8/230°C/450°F.

6. Bake the rolls in the hot oven for about 10–12 minutes, until golden brown. Serve warm with unsalted butter.

THE HERRING SHOULD NOT BE FROZEN. THE BREAD ROLLS
FREEZE WELL

Rack of Lamb with Mint Pesto

3–4 packets of fresh mint leaves (about 50 g/2 oz)
1 packet parsley (about 15 g/½oz)
a pinch of salt
2 garlic cloves, peeled, crushed
50 g/2 oz chopped walnuts
1 tbsp balsamic vinegar
50–75 ml/2–3 fl oz extra virgin olive oil

FOR THE LAMB

2 racks of lamb, each with 8 cutlets, well trimmed

1. For the pesto, combine the first five ingredients in a food processor. Add the balsamic vinegar and process for a couple of seconds. Then add sufficient oil to form a thick paste. Taste for seasoning.

2. Preheat the oven to Gas 6/200°C/400°F and lightly oil a roasting tray.

3. Spread most of the pesto over the meat (on both sides) and place on the roasting tray.

4. Place in the preheated oven and roast for 20 minutes, then remove and rest for about 10 minutes before cutting into individual cutlets. Spoon any of the mint-flavoured juices around the lamb and serve with the mushroom and potato ramekins.

Mushroom and Potato Ramekins

25 g/1 oz unsalted butter
375 g/12 oz button or flat cap mushrooms, wiped,
    finely chopped
1 garlic clove, peeled, crushed
75 ml/3 fl oz double cream
2 tbsp extra virgin olive oil
500 g/1 lb potatoes (about 3 medium-sized),
    peeled, thinly sliced
salt, pepper

1. Heat the butter in a saucepan and gently fry the mushrooms and garlic for 4–5 minutes. Add half of the cream, salt and pepper and cook for a further 5 minutes, uncovered, on a low heat.

2. Meanwhile, heat the oil in a large frying pan and (in batches, if necessary) gently fry the potato slices for about 5 minutes, until well coated and just becoming golden.

3. Preheat the oven to Gas 5/190°C/375°F. Generously butter 4 ramekins (8 cm/3inches).

4. Place a layer of the potatoes in the base of each ramekin, then a layer of the mushroom mixture, then another layer of potatoes. Press down firmly with the back of a spoon, season well, then spoon the remaining cream over the tops. Let them rest for half an hour, press down firmly again, then bake in the preheated oven (on a baking tray) for about 35 minutes, or until the potatoes are tender.

5. Remove from the oven and leave for 10 minutes. Then carefully run a knife around the edges of the ramekins and invert them on to warm plates. (It is easier to place these on the plates before the lamb, as you can turn the plate upside down, to facilitate inverting the ramekins.) If some of the mixture sticks, don't panic: it is easy to re-assemble! (Although the mushroom and potato ramekins cook at a lower temperature than the lamb, simply position them below the meat, and cover loosely with foil, if the top gets brown too quickly.)

THE PESTO FREEZES WELL, BUT NEITHER THE LAMB NOR POTATO
DISH SHOULD BE FROZEN

Hazelnut and Chocolate Fudge Tart

SERVES 8

FOR THE NUT CRUST

125 g/4 oz ground hazelnuts
175 g/6 oz plain flour, sifted
a pinch of salt
125 g/4 oz unsalted butter, melted
1 egg, beaten
40 g/1½ oz golden caster sugar

FOR THE FILLING

50 g/2 oz flaked hazelnuts
175 g/6 oz dark chocolate
175 g/6 oz unsalted butter
175 g/6 oz granulated sugar
40 g/1½ oz plain flour, sifted
a pinch of salt
4 eggs, beaten

1. For the crust, Mix all the ingredients together, until they are well blended. Then press the mixture into a buttered 27 cm/10½-inch flan tin (with removable base). Make sure the mixture goes up the sides too.

2. Chill for at least 30 minutes, or overnight. Preheat the oven to Gas 4/180°C/350°F.

3. Bake the crust for at least 30 minutes or until golden brown. Cool for 30 minutes, while you make the filling.

4. For the filling, scatter the hazelnuts over the baked crust. Melt the chocolate with the butter, in a double boiler or microwave, then cool for about 5 minutes.

5. Mix together the sugar, flour, salt and eggs in a bowl. Whisk or beat with an electric beater for 2 minutes. Stir in the chocolate mixture and combine well.

6. Pour the whole mixture over the flaked hazelnuts in the nut crust and carefully place in the middle of the preheated oven (the same temperature required for the crust) and bake for about 35–40 minutes, until the mixture is just set. Turn off the heat completely and open the oven door fully. Leave the tin inside the oven for about 10 minutes.

7. Remove the tin to a wire rack to cool completely before removing from the tart and cutting into thin slices. (Do not worry if the surface has cracked slightly; dust with a little icing sugar.)

THE TART DOES NOT FREEZE WELL

CHRISTOPHER CHOWN'S consistently high standards at Plas Bode-groes, North Wales, where he is chef-proprietor, have not gone unnoticed. Since opening in 1986, the restaurant has acquired accolades from all the top food guides, including the only Michelin star in Wales. Formerly an accountant, Christopher left his job in 1982 to develop his cooking skills. Naturally gifted as a cook, he allows the fresh taste of essentially local ingredients (such as lamb, lobster and bass) to shine through. Welsh lamb is cooked with mustard and peppers in this beautiful recipe, provided by Christopher.

Roast Best End of Lamb with Mustard and Peppers

2 best ends of lamb, chined and with 6 cutlets each
1 red pepper
1 yellow pepper
1 onion, peeled
2 tbsp wholegrain mustard
2 tbsp honey
a bunch of fresh thyme
olive oil
scasoning
100 ml/3½ fl oz red wine
100 ml/3½ fl oz dark lamb stock

1. Preheat the oven to Gas 6/200°C/400°F.

2. Peel the skin off the lamb, if your butcher has not done so. Trim the upper end of the cutlets and score the fat lightly. Make a paste with the mustard, honey, some of the thyme and some coarsely ground sea salt and pepper.

3. Coat the fat of the best ends with the paste.

4. Chop the peppers and onion into large pieces no smaller than a thumb-nail. Spread these pieces over the base of an enamelled cast-iron pan, large enough to take the 2 best ends. Sprinkle over more thyme and a little olive oil.

5. Place the best ends, paste-side up, over the top of the peppers and roast in the oven for 15–20 minutes, depending on how you like your meat done.

6. Remove the lamb from the pan and rest in a warm place. Add the red wine and stock to the pan and, over a direct heat, stir to release any cooked-on juices and amalgamate the vegetables. Cook briefly until the liquid has almost gone.

7. Carve 3 cutlets for each person and serve the peppers alongside. A good accompaniment is a garlicky potato gratin.

PICKLED HERRING IN SEAWEED

KIPPER FISH-CAKES WITH AVOCADO SAUCE

Seven

THE INGREDIENTS IN THIS MENU ARE BOTH COLOURFUL AND INEXPENSIVE. Kippers, usually served for weekend breakfast or winter tea, are converted into fish-cakes and served with an avocado and caper sauce. The main course is mussels, more often served as a starter, but I like a huge tureen of steaming mussels as a main course, with plenty of home-made bread to 'dunk'. I use home-made mincemeat in the dessert – not as classic mince pies, but layered into a shortcake made from polenta. It is wonderful served with poached dried apricots.

I always buy undyed kippers, which taste exactly the same as dyed but have a more natural colour. They are pale golden brown, as opposed to the bright red colour so often associated with kippers. If you hate the smell of cooked fish lingering around your house, then the old-fashioned method of 'jugging' kippers is ideal. You simply stand them, tail up, in a tall jug, pour in boiling water to cover and leave to stand for about five minutes. This foolproof way also means there is no messy grill or frying pan to clean. In my recipe, you mix them – uncooked – with some cod (or haddock) fillet and mashed potato (a handy item to have in your fridge), then roll them in freshly toasted breadcrumbs and fry. It makes an easy and original starter. The avocado and caper sauce is sharp enough to cut through the oiliness of the kipper.

There is nothing more satisfying than taking home a bucketful of mussels, freshly picked from the beach at low tide, then cooking them very simply with parsley, garlic and wine. We eat them looking over a beautiful sea loch, near the cottage we go to for family holidays, on Scotland's west coast. They somehow seem more succulent than the farmed mussels, but that is pure bias; they are simply fresher. One disadvantage is that wild mussels are always sandier and grittier. Cleaning the mussels is a job which must be done thoroughly, however. Wild mussels should be gathered only from areas where there is no pollution, then, like farmed ones, very carefully picked over: dead mussels (which will not close when tapped lightly) should be thrown away. They must be well scrubbed, and the 'beards' (which are

81

Menu

Kipper Fish-cakes with Avocado Sauce

Mussels in a Chilli Sauce
Barley Bread

Mincemeat Shortcake
with Apricots

like tufts of hair attached to the shells) removed. After cooking, those shells which have remained shut should also be discarded. I like to strain the cooking liquor through muslin, to get rid of any remaining grit or sand.

There are only two fresh chillies used in the sauce, but they are incredibly powerful; in fact, I have taken to wearing thin plastic gloves to protect my hands when I cut chillies. If you forget to wash your hands immediately, and touch your eyes, you will be in agony. I absentmindedly started cutting slivers of raw carrot for the children with the same knife I had just used for slicing fiery red chillies: it nearly put them off raw carrots for life! Unripe chillies are firm and green, whereas ripe ones are red or orange. These are the variety used to make chilli sauces (such as Tabasco) and chilli paste. There is also fresh coriander in the sauce, which is often used with chillies in Middle and Far Eastern cooking. Confusingly, coriander is sometimes known as Chinese parsley and in the States as cilantro. The mussel dish should be accompanied by lots of fresh bread, to mop up the sauce. Barley flour, which, like rye flour, has little gluten, is mixed with wheat flour, to make a wonderful loaf which has a strong earthy flavour.

The shortcake has a coarse, crunchy texture and bright yellow colour, from the polenta. It is handy to make if you have some leftover mincemeat from Christmas. Rich mincemeat lasts for years (it is difficult to say exactly how many; mine is made one year and all gone by the next). If you have no time to make your own, liven up the shop-bought variety by adding some grated apple or carrot, chopped pecans or brazil nuts, freshly grated orange or nutmeg, and copious splashes of rum, Drambuie or brandy. I like to use Hunza apricots (from Afghanistan) which, although fragrant and delicious, do have a stone, so either remove it first or warn your guests.

ADVANCE PREPARATION

The fish-cakes can be refrigerated, uncooked, for 4 hours, but should be fried at the last minute. The mussels can be scrubbed and prepared, but the dish should be freshly cooked. The dessert can be made in the morning, but eaten at room temperature, not straight from the fridge.

WINE SUGGESTIONS

Manzanilla Sherry has the degree of flavour and bite to offset the smokiness of the kipper. Serve a keen-tasting Muscadet with the mussels, and finish with a Tawny Port.

Kipper Fish-cakes with Avocado Sauce

FOR THE FISH-CAKES

150 g/5 oz undyed kipper fillets, cut into pieces
150 g/5 oz cod fillet, cut into pieces
150 g/5 oz firm mashed potatoes
2 tbsp freshly chopped chives
juice of half a lime
freshly ground black pepper
1 egg white
75 g/3 oz fresh breadcrumbs (white or brown),
    toasted lightly until golden brown
2 tbsp groundnut oil

FOR THE SAUCE

1 large ripe avocado, peeled, cut into chunks
1 heaped tbsp capers, well drained
the juice of 1 lime
black pepper

1. Mix together the kippers, cod, potatoes, chives, lime juice and pepper in a food processor. Process only very briefly, so it is a well-combined but not gluey paste.

2. With wet hands, roll the mixture into balls, then flatten into fish-cake shapes. Place in the fridge for at least 30 minutes.

3. Dip each fish-cake into the egg white, then into the breadcrumbs. Chill again for 30 minutes.

4. Meanwhile, make the sauce: purée or blend all the ingredients together until smooth, and season to taste.

5. Heat the oil in a larger frying pan, then when the oil is very hot, fry the fishcakes for about 3 minutes on each side, until golden and crisp. Drain on kitchen paper and serve hot, with some of the sauce.

NONE OF THE STARTER SHOULD BE FROZEN

Mussels in a Chilli Sauce

1.1 kg/2½ lb mussels
150 ml/5 fl oz dry white wine
2 tbsp olive oil
3 garlic cloves, peeled, crushed
4 shallots, peeled, finely chopped
1 large leek, cleaned, finely sliced
2 fresh red chillies, deseeded, chopped
450 ml/¾ pint passata (thick sieved tomatoes)
2 tbsp sun-dried tomatoes in oil, drained, chopped
3 tbsp freshly chopped coriander
2 tbsp freshly chopped parsley

TO SERVE

freshly chopped coriander and parsley, to sprinkle

1. Scrub the mussels well and remove the beards. Discard any which do not close when tapped on a board. Place the mussels in a large saucepan with the wine, bring to the boil, cover and cook over a high heat for about 4–5 minutes, until the shells open. Shake the pan a couple of times, during the cooking. Discard any which remain shut, then strain the liquid through a double layer of muslin into a bowl. Keep the mussels in a dish and the liquid in a jug.

2. Heat the oil in a large pan, then fry the garlic and shallots gently, for about 2 minutes. Then add the leeks and chillies and fry for 3–4 minutes. Increase the heat, add the passata and strained mussel liquor and bring to the boil. Reduce the liquid over a high heat until it starts to thicken, then add the sun-dried tomatoes, coriander and parsley. Lower the heat and cook for a further 2–3 minutes. Season to taste.

3. Replace the mussels, reheat very gently for a couple of minutes, then tip everything carefully into a warmed tureen (or warmed soup bowls) and sprinkle with coriander and parsley. Serve with hunks of warm barley bread.

Barley Bread

450 ml/¾ pint milk
25 g/1 oz fresh yeast
a pinch of sugar
375 g/12 oz barley flour
250 g/8 oz strong white flour
2 tsp salt

TO GLAZE

2 tsp milk

1. Warm the milk to room temperature, then combine it with the yeast and sugar in a large bowl, stirring to dissolve.

2. Add the barley flour, stir then cover. Let the mixture stand for about an hour.

3. Add the white flour and salt and knead until it is smooth (about 10 minutes). The dough will be fairly soft, so have plenty of flour ready to shake on to the dough as you knead.

4. Place in a lightly oiled bowl, cover and let the dough rise for about an hour, in a warm place.

5. Punch down the dough, then cut in 2 and form into 2 round or oval loaves. Place these on 2 greased baking sheets, brush with milk and let them rise again for 30 minutes. Preheat the oven to Gas 9/240°C/475°F.

6. Slash the loaves with a sharp knife across the top, then bake in the centre of a preheated oven for about 20 minutes, until golden brown. Serve warm, with the mussels.

DO NOT FREEZE THE MUSSELS. THE BREAD FREEZES WELL

Mincemeat Shortcake with Apricots

SERVES 8

FOR THE SHORTCAKE

200 g/7 oz plain flour, sifted
325 g/11 oz polenta
1 tsp baking powder
250 g/8 oz caster sugar
250 g/8 oz unsalted butter, cubed
2 eggs, beaten
the grated zest of a large lemon
6–7 tbsp best-quality mincemeat (about 500 g/
    1 lb)

TO SERVE

icing sugar

FOR THE APRICOTS

175 g/6 oz Hunza (or other dried) apricots
300 ml/10 fl oz fresh orange juice

1. Start the day before: soak the apricots in the juice. Next day, preheat the oven to Gas 4/180°C/350°F. Place the fruit and juices in an ovenproof dish, cover and cook in the oven for about 30 minutes. Leave them to cool in their juices.

2. For the shortcake, mix together the flour, polenta, baking powder and sugar in a bowl. Rub in the butter until it resembles fine breadcrumbs.

3. Add the eggs and lemon zest and stir well, to combine.

4. Preheat the oven to Gas 3/160°C/325°F.

5. Press down half of the mixture into a lightly buttered 23 cm/9 inch square cake tin, then carefully spread over the mincemeat. Press the remaining mixture over the top, flattening down gently with the back of a spoon.

6. Place in the preheated oven for about 50–60 minutes, until it is light golden brown at the edges.

7. Allow to cool in the tin, then cut into squares and serve with the poached apricots. (I also like a good dollop of Greek yoghurt or crème fraîche, to make it even more delicious.)

THE DESSERT IS BETTER NOT FROZEN

(Mark Mather)

The menus at chef-patron ANTONY WORRALL THOMPSON'S fashionable restaurants – One Ninety Queen's Gate, Bistrot 190, dell'Ugo and Zoe – all reflect a common theme: 'new-wave' Italian cooking features prominently. He favours gutsy dishes with robust flavours, such as braised lamb shanks with garlic, rosemary and flageolet beans; or mussels with saffron broth and crostini topped with clams. He is a very high-profile chef: he has won many major culinary awards, been a regular contributor to newspapers and magazines, and appeared frequently on radio and television. His recipe for mussels with coriander, greens and lentils is delicious and delightfully easy.

Steamed Mussels with Coriander, Greens and Lentil Broth

SERVES 1 OR 2

1 tbsp olive oil
1 chilli, finely chopped
1 garlic clove, peeled, finely chopped
1 tbsp flour
2 tbsp coriander, chopped
2 tbsp parsley, chopped
4 tbsp dry white wine
5 tbsp fish stock
salt, pepper
10 mussels, scrubbed
a handful of cooked lentils
2 knobs of butter
a small handful of greens (such as carrot tops, beet
   tops, chard)

1. In a large casserole, heat the oil and sauté the onion, chilli and garlic. Add the flour and cook for a minute. Stir in the coriander, parsley, wine and fish stock, salt, pepper.

2. Cover and simmer for 3 minutes; add the mussels and cook for a further 5 minutes, until the mussels open. (Discard any which remain shut.)

3. Remove the mussels to a deep plate and fold in the butter a knob at a time, then the lentils and the greens (they will wilt with the heat).

4. Pour the broth into a separate bowl and serve with the mussels.

Menu

Langoustines with
Lemon Grass Mayonnaise

Chicken with Feta & Tomatoes
Pasta with Rocket

Blackcurrant Tart

Eight

THE FOOD IN THIS MENU IS INTERESTING AND FUN. DEPENDING ON HOW adventurous your guests are, you can serve the langoustines in their shells, on a large plate, reminiscent of a 'fruits de mer platter' served in Breton restaurants. The lemon grass in the mayonnaise livens up a classic accompaniment to seafood. Chicken is so commonplace it is often thought boring, but provided the bird is free-range (not intensively reared), and the accompanying sauce is a little unusual (mine is sun-dried tomatoes and basil) it can be quite delicous. The tart is based on a Finnish recipe for blueberry pie, where the fruit is cooked on an open base similar to a French galette, but with shortcrust rather than puff pastry.

As with many crustaceans, the colder the water the langoustines are fished in, the finer the flavour. My fishmonger obtains his from local ports, such as Port Seton, but there are also fine specimens from the west coast of Scotland. There is often great confusion over terminology: *Nephrops norvegicus* is known not only as langoustine, but also as Norway lobster, Dublin Bay prawn and scampo. Often the langoustine tails are sold alone, for that is where the most delicious meat is found. It is, however, worth cracking open the claws in larger langoustines as there is also very good eating there. If you are serving them in their shells, I would garnish only with some lemon, to squeeze. I think it makes for a very convivial evening, with everyone eating messily with their fingers. In Sweden and Finland, crayfish parties can notoriously be excuses for insobriety, as guests drink Schnapps throughout. Fresh dill flavours the water the crayfish are cooked in, so the juices, drunk from the shells, are subtly flavoured with dill. The only accompaniment I had at Finnish crayfish parties (where they have huge customised napkins to tie round your neck) was toast or bread with butter, and plenty of extra dill. Similarly, when you are serving the freshly boiled langoustines, perhaps provide fresh bread and unsalted butter with the aromatic mayonnaise. If you feel the need, shell the crustaceans for your guests by twisting the tail off the body, removing the shell and carefully pulling out the dark intestinal thread.

On to a slightly less messy main course, where chicken breasts are stuffed with feta cheese and sun-dried tomatoes and served with a sauce of the tomatoes with basil. A jar of sun-dried tomatoes (marinated in oil) is handy to have in the larder. I throw the tomatoes into pasta, risotto, fresh tomato sauce, ratatouille, sandwiches: their intense flavour enhances most dishes which call for fresh tomatoes to be cooked. If you buy them dry (not marinated), soak them in warm water for an hour, then drain very well on kitchen paper. Pop them into a jar with a little salt, cover with extra virgin olive oil or herb-flavoured olive oil and a few sprigs of fresh thyme or rosemary. If they are well sealed they will keep for a couple of months in a cool larder. Fresh pasta is tossed with some rocket (which is also – confusingly – known as rucola, roquette and arugula) for a very simple accompaniment.

Open fruit pies, made on flat baking trays rather than within the confines of the edges of a tart tin, are commonplace in Finland in summertime. Blueberries, lingonberries or rhubarb are used to top a rich crusty base. They are usually served cold, with afternoon coffee; I prefer this blackcurrant tart, which has a sweet short pastry and a sharp, tangy filling, to be served still warm from the oven, with a dollop of Greek yoghurt.

ADVANCE PREPARATION

The langoustines can be cooked several hours in advance, and kept cold; the mayonnaise can be made the day before and stirred just before serving. The chicken can be stuffed a couple of hours before cooking, then refrigerated. The pasta can be made earlier in the day, covered loosely with baking paper and refrigerated. (Do not cover with clingfilm.) The tart can be made in advance and reheated in a low oven.

WINE SUGGESTIONS

Before the meal serve your guests Seppelt, Méthode Champenoise, Salinger, or another high quality Australian or New Zealand sparkling white wine, or indeed a sparkling Saumur. Make sure there is enough left over to serve with the pudding. With the chicken, try a Barbera, or a Californian Zinfandel.

Langoustines with Lemon Grass Mayonnaise

12–16 live langoustines (about 65–75 g/2½–3 oz
   each), cleaned
½ tsp salt

FOR THE MAYONNAISE

1 tbsp finely chopped fresh lemon grass (about 1
   plump stalk, outer leaves removed)
1 egg
1 tbsp squeezed lemon juice
125–150 ml/4–5 fl oz groundnut oil
50–75 ml/2–3 fl oz extra virgin olive oil
salt, pepper

1. To cook the langoustines, bring a very large saucepan filled with water
   and the salt to the boil. (Bear in mind that the langoustines should be
   completely covered, so you will need a lot of water; do in 2 batches if
   necessary).

2. Once it is fiercely boiling, quickly throw in the langoustines, and allow
   the water to come back fully to the boil again. Let them cook for about
   1–2 minutes – no longer – then drain and plunge into cold water to stop
   the cooking process. Once they are cold, dry them and serve with the
   mayonnaise, suitable implements for claw-cracking and finger-bowls.

3. For the mayonnaise, place the finely chopped lemon grass (once you
   have removed the outer leaves, chop only the plump lower part of the
   stem) in a food processor with the egg, and process for 30 seconds.

4. Add the lemon juice and process for a further 10 seconds. Then, with the machine running, slowly pour in the oils through the feeder tube – add sufficient to give the correct consistency for mayonnaise. Season to taste with salt and pepper.

NONE OF THE STARTER SHOULD BE FROZEN

Chicken with Feta and Tomatoes

150 g/5 oz feta cheese, crumbled
2 tbsp sun-dried tomatoes, roughly chopped
4 large basil leaves, shredded
freshly ground black pepper
4 large (free-range) chicken breasts, boned, unskinned
a little oil from the jar of sun-dried tomatoes (make sure it is extra virgin olive oil)

FOR THE SAUCE

2 garlic cloves, peeled, crushed
2 tbsp oil, taken from the jar of sun-dried tomatoes (extra virgin olive oil)
3 tbsp sun-dried tomatoes
6–8 large basil leaves
$\frac{1}{2}$ tbsp balsamic vinegar
150 ml/5 fl oz chicken stock
salt/pepper

TO SERVE

fresh basil sprigs

LANGOUSTINES WITH LEMON GRASS MAYONNAISE

OXTAIL WITH GREMOLATA

1. For the chicken, mix together the cheese, tomatoes, basil and pepper (feta is a very salty cheese, so do not add salt) with the back of a spoon until it resembles a thick paste. Preheat the oven to Gas7/220°C/425°F.

2. Carefully separate the skin from the top of each breast (without detaching the skin completely) and spread the cheese mixture under the skin. Then replace the skin, patting carefully with your hand, so the cheese mixture is completely covered. Pour a little of the oil from the jar into a saucer and, dipping in a pastry brush, brush the chicken with some of the oil.

3. Place the chicken in the middle of the preheated oven for about 20 minutes, or until the chicken is just cooked. (To test, pierce the breast with a sharp knife; the juices should run clear.)

4. Meanwhile, make the sauce. Fry the garlic gently in the oil for 2–3 minutes, then tip the garlic and oil into a food processor, adding all the other ingredients. Whizz everything until it is well blended, then season to taste with salt and pepper.

5. Transfer the sauce to a saucepan and gently heat through, until piping hot.

6. To serve, place the chicken on the warmed serving plate (you can cut it in slices with a very sharp knife if you like) and spoon some of the tomato and basil sauce around. Garnish with fresh basil.

Pasta with Rocket

250 g/8 oz strong white flour
1 tsp salt
2 large eggs
25 g/1 oz rocket leaves
1 tbsp extra virgin olive oil

1. Combine the first three ingredients in a food processor, then briefly knead the mixture together with your hands. Cover with clingfilm and place in the fridge for a minimum of half an hour.

2. Roll out the pasta to the penultimate setting on a pasta machine, then let the sheets rest, uncovered, for 15–20 minutes. (This facilitates cutting.)

3. Cut the pasta into tagliatelle, then dry for 15–20 minutes. Cook in boiling salted water for no more than 1 minute.

4. Shred the rocket (making sure any coarse stalks are removed) and toss into the freshly drained pasta, with the olive oil. Season with plenty of black pepper and serve at once in a warmed bowl.

THE CHICKEN SHOULD NOT BE FROZEN. THE PASTA CAN BE FROZEN AND SHOULD BE COOKED WITHOUT THAWING, FOR AN EXTRA MINUTE

Blackcurrant Tart

SERVES 6

FOR THE PASTRY

150 g/5 oz unsalted butter, softened
50 g/2 oz caster sugar
1 egg, beaten
250 g/8 oz plain flour, sifted
2 tbsp double cream
a pinch of salt
1 egg white, to brush
caster sugar, to sprinkle

FOR THE FILLING

500 g/1 lb blackcurrants
75 g/3 oz caster sugar
1 tbsp semolina

TO SERVE

Greek yoghurt

1. For the pastry, cream the butter and sugar together until light and fluffy.

2. Add the egg and stir well to combine. Gradually add the flour, salt and the cream a little at a time, until well mixed. (Be careful not to work the dough too much or it will be tough.)

3. Roll out a large, wide sheet of clingfilm and place the dough in the middle. Place a second sheet of clingfilm on the top and roll out the pastry with a rolling pin, until you have a thin circle, about 30–33 cm/

12–13 inches in diameter. Remove the pastry, in the clingfilm, to the fridge for at least an hour. Preheat the oven to Gas 6/200°C/400°F.

4. For the fruit, mix together the blackcurrants with the sugar and semolina.

5. Peel away one sheet of clingfilm and place the pastry on to a lightly buttered baking tray. Peel away the top sheet of clingfilm. Place the fruit mixture in the middle, then spread it out to about 4 cm/1½ inches from the edge. Fold in the dough a little, to form a crust all around. (Most of the fruit should be showing; the crust should only cover a little of the fruit at the sides.) Brush all round the crust with egg white, then sprinkle with caster sugar.

6. Bake in the preheated oven for about 30 minutes, until the crust is golden brown. Cool for about 10 minutes, then cut and serve, still warm with thick Greek yoghurt.

THE TART CAN BE FROZEN THEN REHEATED ONCE THAWED

BETTY ALLEN, owner of The Airds Hotel, Port Appin, with her husband Eric, is a self-taught chef whose cooking is among the finest in Scotland. Their charming hotel, situated on the edge of the beautiful Loch Linnhe, is one of the most welcoming in the country. Betty cooks in a sophisticated, yet unpretentious manner, to bring out the natural intensity of local flavours. Her recipe for chicken breasts filled with mushrooms is absolutely delicious and delightfully easy to produce.

Chicken Breasts filled with Mushrooms

SERVES 8

8 chicken breasts, skin removed
4 shallots, peeled, finely chopped
1 garlic clove, peeled, finely chopped
a few leaves of tarragon or other fresh herb
750 g/1½ lb mushrooms, chopped
1 egg
4–6 tbsp double cream
butter
salt, pepper, grated nutmeg
(clingfilm)

1. Sauté the shallots and garlic until soft, then remove to a plate and put in the fridge until quite cold.

2. Sauté the mushrooms and sprinkle with a little grated nutmeg. When soft, remove from the pan and drain off all the liquid, then transfer to a plate and put in the fridge and leave until quite cold.

3. Remove the 'loose' fillets attached to each chicken breast and pull out the sinew. (This meat should weigh 250 g/8 oz altogether.) Chop up these fillet pieces (keeping the 8 large fillets whole) and put into a food processor with the egg, mushrooms, shallots and garlic and a little salt and pepper.

101

4. Put the chicken mixture through a sieve and, using a hand-held electric blender, add about 4 tbsp cream, beating it into the chicken mixture. Add more cream if necessary to make the mixture slightly sloppy. Add the tarragon, taste and season.

5. Cut a slit the length of each breast, to make a deep socket. Fill with the mixture and gently pull the edges together. Lay the filled breast on a piece of clingfilm and roll up fairly firmly, to make a thick sausage. Leave in the fridge until they are quite firm.

6. When ready to cook, put them into a pan which contains hot water about 5 cm/2 inches deep. Barely simmer for 10–12 minutes, until only just firm in the centre, turning halfway during cooking. Remove and leave in the clingfilm until you slice them just before required.

Nine

THERE IS NO DOUBT ABOUT WHEN TO COOK THIS COMFORTING WARMING menu: winter is not only the best time of the year for mussels, it is also the time when appetites crave wholesome and hearty casseroles, such as oxtail, and filling puddings such as the pear and ginger steamed pudding.

The starter is a light crêpe made with a mixture of buckwheat and plain flour, which is rolled round some freshly cooked mussels in a sauce spiked with saffron and orange. Although you are serving the mussels out of their shells, the liquid you cook them in is incorporated into the sauce. Be very cautious when adding saffron threads: using too many will soon make you a pauper (it is the most expensive spice in the world); it will also give a horrific packet-custard yellow hue to your erstwhile delicate sauce. To use saffron strands, soak a generous pinch in either warm water or the liquid you will cook with – in this case, the mussel liquor. The buckwheat flour in the crêpes (typical of Breton galettes and crêpes) adds a savoury, almost nutty flavour to the dish.

Oxtail is an inexpensive meat which makes the most delicious, nourishing casserole. It is a very fatty meat, so should be well trimmed of fat and cut into 5 cm/2 inch pieces. (It is often sold already jointed.) I like the contrasting sweetness of redcurrant jelly in the sauce – it also makes the colour a deep rich red. I enjoy mixing redcurrants with crab-apples when I make redcurrant jelly. Since I pick vast quantities of currants from a friend's splendid fruit garden, I freeze many, to use when crab-apples are in season later on in the year (September and October are best for them). I use about two-thirds redcurrants to one-third crab-apples. The good thing about crab-apples, which are so small they can be a nuisance to prepare, is that you need only wash them, then throw them in your jelly pan with the currants. By straining the pulp through the jelly bag you eliminate all the cores and peel, and also the stalks from the redcurrants. Apart from adding an essential hint of sweetness to many gravies and sauces, redcurrant jelly is also wonderful on sweet scones or used to glaze strawberry tarts. I also like to mix a couple of teaspoons with the butter or oil in the frying pan when I

Menu

Mussels in Buckwheat Crêpes

Oxtail with Gremolata
Celeriac Purée

Steamed Ginger & Pear Pudding

am browning lamb chops or venison steaks, for added flavour.

Gremolata, which is a mixture of parsley, lemon zest and garlic, is usually added (at the end of cooking) to the famous Milanese dish, *ossobuco*, made with veal shin-bones. It is excellent to cut through any potential fattiness of oxtail casserole – and adds a beautiful bright colour.

Celeriac is becoming more commonly used in Britain nowadays. It is the root of a variety of celery, whose unappealing exterior belies its creamy-white, celery-flavoured flesh. The purée is also good with any game dish.

The pudding is a steamed sponge flavoured with ginger syrup (from a jar of stem ginger) and topped with some finely chopped stem ginger and slices of pear. Stem ginger adds lots of flavour – and texture – to ice-creams, cakes, cheesecakes and biscuits. I find the easiest way to chop it is to fish it out of the jar with a fork, then hold it in place with the fork, while you chop with a sharp knife. Do not waste any of the precious syrup it is preserved in – pour it over vanilla ice-cream, or add it to stewed rhubarb or sweet custards. For the pears, I would suggest using either Doyenne du Comice or William's Bon Chrétien, which can be lightly cooked or eaten raw, as they are both juicy and sweet.

ADVANCE PREPARATION

The crêpes can be prepared and refrigerated for up to two hours in advance. The oxtail can be made the day before (any fat skimmed off) and gently reheated. The gremolata should be added at the last minute. The pudding should be steamed on the day.

WINE SUGGESTIONS

Muscadet, or another light dry white wine, should be offered with the mussel crêpes. The rich taste of the oxtail will be well matched with either Barolo or Chianti Classico. Finish with Bual Madeira.

Mussels in Buckwheat Crêpes

FOR THE CRÊPE BATTER

65 g/2½ oz plain flour, sifted
40 g/1½ oz buckwheat flour
a pinch of salt
1 egg
300 ml/10 fl oz milk

FOR THE MUSSELS

1 kg/2 lb mussels, debearded, scrubbed (you want
    about 6–8 per person, but have more, as some
    may not open up on cooking)
150 ml/5 fl oz dry white wine
a generous pinch of saffron strands
25 g/1 oz butter
25 g/1 oz plain flour
150 ml/5 fl oz double cream
the grated zest of 1 small orange
salt, pepper
1 tbsp milk

1. First make the crêpe batter. Either whisk everything together or blend in a food processor until you have a smooth batter. Place in a bowl, cover, and refrigerate for an hour.

2. Meanwhile, ensure the mussels are well scrubbed and discard any with broken shells or any that do not close when tapped.

3. Place the wine in a saucepan, add the mussels, bring to the boil and cook, covered, for 4–5 minutes. Sieve the liquid through muslin and retain. Discard any mussels which have not opened. Shell the others and set aside.

4. Soak the saffron in the mussel liquor and leave for about 15 minutes, while you make the crêpes. Using a piece of kitchen paper rubbed in butter, wipe a hot crêpe pan, pour in a little of the batter and make the crêpes – you need 8. (The mixture makes about 10.) Stack them on a plate, one on top of the other. (Although I never bother, you can put greaseproof paper between them.) Preheat the oven to Gas 4/180°C/350°F.

5. For the sauce, melt the butter, then add the flour, stirring to make a roux. Add the saffron/mussel liquor and, whisking all the time, bring to the boil, then reduce to a simmer. Stir in the cream, orange zest and salt and pepper to taste, then simmer for a couple of minutes.

6. Place 8 crêpes on a flat board. Top each with 3–4 mussels. Spoon some of the sauce over each, leaving about 1 tbsp over. Roll up the crêpes, to enclose the filling, then carefully remove them to a buttered ovenproof dish (oblong-shaped, so they are all side by side). Thin down the remaining sauce with the milk and drizzle this over the crêpes.

7. Heat them through in the preheated oven for about 15–20 minutes and serve piping hot, on warmed plates.

THE UNFILLED CRÊPES CAN BE FROZEN. DEFROST WELL BEFORE ROLLING ROUND THE FILLING

Oxtail with Gremolata

1.25 kg/3 lb oxtail, cut into 5 cm/2 inch pieces
½ tbsp olive oil
1 large onion, peeled, finely chopped
1 leek, sliced
2 carrots, peeled chopped
300 g/10 oz turnip (swede), peeled, chopped
2 sticks of celery, chopped
150 ml/5 fl oz red wine
1½ tbsp tomato purée
600 ml/1 pint oxtail or beef stock
1 large sprig each of rosemary and thyme
½ tsp salt
black pepper
1 heaped tbsp redcurrant jelly

FOR THE GREMOLATA

the finely grated zest of 1 lemon
1 heaped tbsp freshly chopped parsley
1 garlic clove, peeled, crushed

1. Trim the oxtail of most of the fat, then heat a large heavy casserole until very hot, without adding any fat. Brown the oxtail pieces in the casserole, turning them so they do not stick, then remove with a slotted spoon. Preheat the oven to Gas 3/160°C/325°F.

2. Add the oil to the casserole, then fry the onions gently for a couple of minutes. Add the leeks, carrots, turnip and celery. Fry these gently for about 5 minutes, until they are just softened.

3. Remove them with a slotted spoon, then increase the heat and add the red wine. Stir to deglaze the pan, scraping up all the caramelised bits. Reduce the liquid to about half.

4. Reduce the heat while you replace all the vegetables and oxtail to the casserole. Add the tomato purée, stock, herbs, salt and pepper. Bring to the boil, cover, then remove to the preheated oven for about 3 hours, stirring every hour.

5. Remove from the oven, and, using a slotted spoon, remove the meat and vegetables to a warm dish. Place the casserole on a direct heat, then add the redcurrant jelly. Stirring well, reduce the liquid over a high heat, until it is slightly thickened. Taste for seasoning, then replace the meat and vegetables, reheating gently if necessary.

6. To serve, mix all the gremolata ingredients together, then sprinkle over the oxtail. Offer the celeriac purée separately.

Celeriac Purée

500 g/1 lb peeled celeriac (weight after peeling)
250 g/8 oz peeled potatoes (weight after peeling)
25 g/1 oz butter, softened
100 ml/3½ fl oz crème fraîche
salt, black pepper

1. Cut the vegetables into small pieces, then cook them in a saucepan of boiling salted water, until they are tender (about 15 minutes).

2. Drain them well and mash them with a potato masher or pass them through a mouli-légume.

3. Add the softened butter and crème fraîche, beat well, then season to taste with salt and pepper and serve at once.

THE OXTAIL CAN BE FROZEN, WITHOUT THE GREMOLATA. DO NOT FREEZE THE PURÉE

Steamed Ginger and Pear Pudding

SERVES 6

FOR THE TOPPING

50 g/2 oz unsalted butter
1 large pear, peeled, cored, thinly sliced
1½ tbsp stem ginger, chopped
75 g/3 oz soft brown sugar
125 ml/4 fl oz double cream

FOR THE STEAMED PUDDING

125 g/4 oz unsalted butter, softened
125 g/4 oz caster sugar
2 large eggs, beaten
175 g/6 oz self-raising four, sifted
2 tbsp ginger syrup, from the jar of stem ginger
a pinch of salt

1. For the topping, melt the butter in a saucepan and add the pears. Gently cook for about a minute, then remove with a slotted spoon. Add the chopped ginger to the pears and keep aside.

2. Add the soft brown sugar to the melted butter, then the cream, and bring slowly to the boil. Simmer for about 5 minutes, then remove from the heat.

3. For the pudding, cream the butter and the sugar together until pale and light. Then beat in the eggs, one at a time. Fold in the flour gradually, then lastly add the ginger syrup and salt. Ensure it is all well mixed.

4. Butter a 1 litre/1¾ pints bowl (suitable for steaming) and spoon in the pears and ginger, then about two-thirds of the sauce. Carefully spoon in

the pudding mixture, over the pears and ginger sauce. (Do this in small spoonfuls, not in one large dollop.)

5. Cover the bowl with buttered, double baking parchment or foil, in which you have folded over a pleat in the middle (to allow room for expansion). Tie securely with string (I find it easier to tie a string 'handle' too, for easy removal) and steam in a large saucepan of simmering water for about 2 hours. Keep checking and topping up the water-level every half hour or so.

6. Reheat the remaining sauce, and serve with the pudding. Invert it carefully on to a warmed serving dish, letting the pears and ginger pour down the sides. Offer pouring cream or thin custard separately.

DAVID ADLARD discovered his love of cooking later in life than most chefs: he left the boardroom for the kitchen at the age of 30. He opened his restaurant, Adlard's, in Norwich in 1983 with his wife Mary, and since then he has never looked back. His accomplished cooking is often described as 'modern French', where the emphasis is on good ingredients which are effectively and simply combined. His puddings display the same assured careful preparation as his other courses. David's recipe for Apple Charlotte with Cinnamon Ice-Cream is infallible – and also quite delicious.

Apple Charlotte and Cinnamon Ice-Cream

FOR THE CHARLOTTE

500 g/1 lb Bramley apples
sugar
lemon juice
nutmeg, cinnamon
white bread (preferably brioche: the bread must be
    firm)
butter for sautéeing
clarified butter, to soak the bread

1. Peel and cut the apples into 1 cm/½ inch cubes. Sauté them quickly in the butter, so the apples do not go brown. Add sugar, cinnamon and nutmeg, to taste. Leave the apples rather undercooked as they are to be further cooked in the charlotte.

2. Line the base of a small pudding mould with greaseproof paper. Cut the bread into 3mm /⅛ inch thickness, then soak them in the clarified butter and line the mould. Then press the apples in firmly, pressing down hard. Cover the apple with bread and then cover the pudding mould with foil.

112

WARM ARTICHOKE BREAD WITH TOMATO SALAD

BRAMBLE CLAFOUTIS

3. Cook in a very hot preheated oven (Gas 7/220°C/425°F) for 20 minutes. After 15 minutes, examine the side of the charlotte, to check if the bread is brown. If so, remove from the oven.

4. Once it is cooked, pour a pool of crème anglaise (see below) on to the base of a plate, then demould the charlotte on top. Serve at once with the ice-cream.

FOR THE ICE-CREAM

300 ml/10 fl oz double cream
300 ml/10 fl oz milk
1 cinnamon stick, broken up
half a vanilla pod
75 g/3 oz sugar
6 egg yolks

1. Infuse the milk and cream with the cinnamon and vanilla.

2. Make a crème anglaise with the infused milk and cream. When it is cool, churn it in an ice-cream machine.

Menu

Warm Artichoke Bread
with Tomato Salad

Fresh Pasta with
Wild Mushrooms & Cream

Quince Compote

Ten

THIS IS A FAVOURITE MENU OF MINE, AS IT HAS SIMPLE, BOLD FLAVOURS AND textures. The starter is a type of thick-based pizza, topped with chunks of artichokes marinated in oil, and crème fraîche. It is served warm with the easiest salad possible, a tomato salad. The fresh pasta is flavoured with thyme and sauced with an abundance of wild mushrooms – fresh and dried (some cultivated can be substituted, depending on the season) – and some cream, parmesan and garlic. The rich mushrooms and their meaty texture will have even the most intransigent carnivore begging for more. I like quince to round off this menu of favourite ingredients. In my list of Desert Island Dishes, I would choose quince. Although I have eaten them on rare occasions, each time is like a Proustian flashback – I can remember details of time and place vividly: that must be true love!

For the starter, the bread dough is made like a pizza with good Italian flour and olive oil. The topping is a mixture of artichoke hearts, which are marinated in oil, and are commonly served as an Italian antipasto, often with a selection of smoked meats, salami, olives or mushrooms in oil. Jars of the artichokes (*carciofini*) are available from many supermarkets and delicatessens. They can also be tossed into pasta, with some freshly chopped herbs and crème fraîche, or layered into Mediterranean-style picnic loaves, made with ciabatta, salami, basil and tomatoes. Try to buy sun-ripened tomatoes for the salad. Their flavour is unquestionably superior to watery greenhouse offerings.

When I lived in Finland, my first weekend outing was into one of the country's many forests to hunt for mushrooms. As I had only been used to button mushrooms from the greengrocers, this was a unique experience. Mushroom-gathering is not merely of culinary interest, it is also a social occasion. Just as in winter the Finns meet on the cross-country ski track, in autumn they get together to pick mushrooms. We found Saffron milk caps (*Lactarius deliciosus*) which grow near pine or spruce trees. My Finnish friend Ritva dries them in the autumn, for use throughout the year. She makes a wonderfully simple mushroom salad (*sienisalaatti*) with fresh wild mush-

115

rooms, lemon, shallots and sour cream. Other wild mushrooms suitable for my pasta recipe are morels (*morchella*). This is one of the most prized fungi, which appear from March to May. Fresh or dried, they are both dreadfully expensive, but their intense earthy flavour make them well worth the money. Chanterelles (*Cantharellus cibarius*) are delicious in a mixed mushroom sauce, as well as ceps (*Boletus edulis*). The latter have a bold, almost meaty flavour, while chanterelles are more delicate and fragrant. In this recipe, it is not too crucial which species of fresh or dried mushrooms you use; you can also add some cultivated ones such as strong, nutty chestnut mushrooms, meaty-textured shiitake or the more delicately flavoured oyster mushrooms. But I would insist on at least 25 g/1 oz dried wild mushrooms, and try to have some dried morels, as the crowning glory. I like to add some fresh thyme to the pasta, but you could also add fresh parsley. The pasta dish is exquisite on its own (the only trouble is that there is never enough), but offer a crisp green salad, with a vinaigrette of olive oil and sherry vinegar, before the dessert.

The first time I had quince was in Paris, when a friend, Sabine, brought me some from her home in the Pyrenees. Having removed the luscious fruit a couple of hours beforehand, her bag was still filled with the lingering, alluring, fragrant scent of quince. I was later able to indulge my recently found passion in Sydney, where they are more plentiful than in this country. Cooking them long and slow means they become a brilliant ruby-red colour but still retain their haunting flavour. All you need to serve is a generous spoonful of mascarpone cheese, whipped with a little sugar and a dash of quince eau-de-vie (to mix into the mascarpone, but also to drink!).

ADVANCE PREPARATIONS

The bread can be made in advance and reheated. The tomato salad should be freshly prepared. The fresh pasta can be made earlier, loosely covered with baking parchment and kept in the fridge, until cooking. The mushrooms should be cooked just before eating. The quince is best straight from the oven.

WINE SUGGESTIONS

The woodsmokey richness of Barolo lends itself to the autumnal flavour of the wild mushrooms and it can equally well be served with the tomato salad.

Moscatel de Valencia, or Riesling Spatlese, will not overpower the delicate perfume of the quince.

Warm Artichoke Bread with Tomato Salad

WARM ARTICHOKE BREAD

500 g/1 lb OO flour (or strong white flour)
1 tsp salt
25 g/1 oz fresh yeast
a pinch of sugar
275–300 ml/9–10 fl oz tepid water
2 tbsp olive oil (or oil from the jar of marinated
    artichokes), plus oil for brushing
100 ml/3½ fl oz crème fraîche
3 egg yolks
salt, pepper
1 jar (275 g/9oz) of artichokes marinated in oil,
    sliced
freshly chopped rosemary and thyme, to sprinkle

1. Sift the flour and salt into a large bowl. Dissolve the yeast with the sugar in a quarter of the tepid water. Stir and leave for about 10 minutes.

2. Pour this on to the flour, with the oil and sufficient tepid water to produce a soft dough. Knead the dough for about 10 minutes, then place the dough in an oiled bowl, cover and let it rise in a warm place for about 1 hour.

3. Preheat the oven to Gas 7/220°C/425°F.

4. Knock back the dough, then press into an oiled swiss-roll tin (23 × 33 cm/9 × 13 inches), making sure it is of equal thickness all over, and pressing it up the sides. Brush lightly with olive oil.

117

smooth dough is formed. Cover with clingfilm and refrigerate for 30 minutes.

2. Pass the dough through a pasta machine (as described in Chapter 8) and cut into tagliatelle.

3. For the sauce, soak all the dried mushrooms in the wine for 30 minutes. Then drain them through a muslin-lined sieve, reserving the liquid. Place the 8 morels in a saucepan with 2–3 tbsp of the liquid.

4. Roughly chop all the other mushrooms, if necessary. Heat the oil in a large saucepan, add the shallots and garlic and fry for 2–3 minutes. Add the (soaked) dried and fresh mushrooms and fry gently for about 3–4 minutes.

5. Add the reserved mushroom liquor, bring to the boil, then reduce the heat and simmer, uncovered, until most of the liquid has evaporated.

6. Add the cream and simmer for a further 5 minutes. Meanwhile, gently heat the morels in their saucepan, simmering for 4–5 minutes.

7. Cook the tagliatelle in boiling salted water for no more than a minute, then drain well.

8. Remove the mushroom sauce from the heat and stir in the parmesan, then taste for seasoning. Add salt and pepper to taste.

9. Toss in the freshly cooked pasta to the sauce and gently combine, ensuring it is all well coated.

10. Serve at once on warmed plates. Place one of the reserved morels on top, then decorate with a few shavings of parmesan.

THE PASTA CAN BE FROZEN. DO NOT DEFROST, BUT ADD ON AN EXTRA MINUTE TO COOKING TIME. DO NOT FREEZE THE SAUCE

Quince Compote

3–4 medium-sized quince
the juice of 1 lemon
150 g/5 oz caster sugar
300 ml/10 fl oz Sauternes or other light, sweet wine
150 ml/5 fl oz water
1 vanilla pod, split

TO SERVE

mascarpone cheese whipped with a little sieved
    icing sugar, to taste (and some quince
    eau-de-vie)

1. Preheat the oven to Gas1/140°C/275°F. Peel the quince, cut them into fairly thick slices and lay them in a baking dish.

2. Squeeze over the lemon juice, to prevent discolouration. Then spinkle over the sugar, add the Sauternes, water and vanilla pod. Cover the dish tightly then bake in the preheated oven for about 2½ hours or until the quince are ruby-red and the liquid is thick and syrupy.

3. Allow the fruit to cool in their juices and serve at room temperature, with large spoonfuls of the mascarpone.

DO NOT FREEZE THE COMPOTE

(Christopher Hill Photographic)

PAUL RANKINE's restaurant in the heart of Belfast has changed Ulster's hitherto grim culinary reputation. Six months after opening Roscoff in 1990, Paul (with his Canadian wife Jeanne) earned Northern Ireland's first Michelin star. His cooking is eclectic and modern, showing influences from the many places he and Jeanne have lived and eaten – there are elements of Italian, Californian, Asian, French and Irish styles in his cooking. Having also worked under Albert Roux, Paul has not forgotten the strong classical roots of *haute cuisine*. Here is one of his inventive recipes for a quite outstanding vegetarian pasta dish.

Pappardelle with Artichokes, Girolles and a Basil Pesto

FOR THE PAPPARDELLE

250 g/8 oz unbleached strong flour
2 large eggs
1 tsp olive oil
a pinch of salt

1. Mix all the ingredients in a food processor or mixer. The dough should come together well, but not be soft or damp. Using a pasta machine, roll the dough to less than 3 mm/$\frac{1}{8}$ inch in thickness (the last notch of most machines). By hand, cut the pieces into strips each about 2.5–4 cm/1–1$\frac{1}{2}$ inches wide.

FOR THE BASIL PESTO

4 cups of fresh basil leaves
2 tbsp pine nuts
2 garlic cloves, peeled
125 g/4 oz freshly grated parmesan
125 ml/4 fl oz olive oil
salt, pepper

2. Place all the ingredients into the food processor and process until the pesto is well blended. Transfer to a bowl.

FOR THE ARTICHOKES AND GIROLLES

2–3 fresh artichokes
lemon juice
olive oil
2–3 handfuls of fresh wild mushrooms, such as
    girolles (yellow chanterelles)
salt, pepper

3. For the artichokes, carefully trim the leaves from the artichokes with a sharp knife. Then, using a spoon, scrape out the hairy choke, and slice each heart into 12 segments. Drizzle the cut artichokes with a little lemon juice, to prevent discolouration. Sauté the pieces in a little olive oil for about 5 minutes, until they are tender. Set aside.

4. Carefully trim and clean the mushrooms and then simply sauté them over a high heat in a little olive oil, and season with salt and pepper.

5. To assemble, cook the pasta strips in a large pot of boiling salted water for several minutes or until *al dente*. Drain well in a colander.

6. Divide the pasta on to 4 warmed plates and spoon the artichokes and mushrooms over the top, followed by a few generous tablespoons of pesto. Serve immediately, with a bowl of freshly grated parmesan on the side.

Menu

Warm Goat's Cheese Salad

Rabbit with Black Olive Paste
Braised Borlotti Beans

Bramble Clafoutis

Eleven

OLIVE OIL FEATURES STRONGLY IN THIS MENU. THERE IS A SALAD WITH A grilled goat's cheese, which has been marinated in olive oil. The rabbit is cooked in a powerful black olive sauce, made from a black olive paste similar to tapenade. And the borlotti beans are finished off with a drizzle of fruity olive oil. Luckily the dessert is a creamy fruity concoction, without the merest suggestion of oil!

I used to dislike olive oil because of its rather greasy aftertaste, until I discovered extra virgin. This oil, the purest of the cold-pressed, usually has a fruity flavour and fine fragrance, although different oils vary from country to country and from grove to grove: some taste stronger and heavier. In Edinburgh there is a well-known Italian food shop, Valvona and Crolla. I often dash in for a small package of fresh yeast or some parmesan cheese, and end up having a full-blown olive oil tasting with a member of staff, dipping freshly baked bread into different extra virgin oils, then probably buying at least two bottles of the tastiest . . . I can never decide!

The goat's cheese used for the starter I marinate in olive oil, with some herbs, to give them extra depth of flavour and to keep them moist. I use fresh goat's cheeses from the Isle of Gigha, off the west coast of Scotland. These do not have a rind, as they are not mature cheeses. They should be drained on kitchen paper to absorb any excess moisture, then placed in a jar (I do four or five at a time) with some sprigs of rosemary, tarragon or fresh bay leaves, then covered with your best olive oil. In the winter months, you will have to bring the jar into the warmth for the oil to 'melt' – it usually solidifies in a cold larder. The cheeses will keep for a couple of months and can be eaten as they are, or grilled and served with a salad. I like the classic combination of walnuts with goat's cheese, so I use some walnut oil in the salad dressing. There will be lots of plate-wiping, to lap up all the delicious oils, so provide plenty of good crusty bread.

My first happy rabbit-eating memories were of Provence when I was an au pair, where a meal started with a strongly flavoured mousse made from the rabbits' livers, then the most delicious rabbit dish cooked in a good-quality red wine. Well, I thought it was the most delicious until I was given, the following week, rabbit cooked in a white wine, with a host of golden garlic cloves. I seem to remember lavender was also involved in the dish, as there were lavender fields all around. Since those days, I have enjoyed many a luscious *lapin*, but a particular favourite is cooked with a form of tapenade, the Provencal paste made with black olives, anchovies, tuna and olive oil. I miss out the tuna and add a couple of extra ingredients for my rabbit recipe. Any leftover paste will keep well in the fridge to spread on toasted bread which can then be topped with some feta or goat's cheese, or some slivers of roasted peppers or sun-dried tomatoes. You can use either wild or farmed rabbit for this recipe, but the wild has a more gamey flavour (farmed tastes rather like chicken) so the whole flavour is very strong, which does not appeal to everyone. It is accompanied by little croutons of toasted bread spread with some of the olive paste. A dish of slowly braised borlotti beans is thick enough to soak up the rabbit juices.

The dessert is a variation of the classical French dish, which French friends used to bake. They used either black cherries, or prunes steeped in Armagnac, but I like the flavour of Scottish brambles (blackberries) in this light sweet batter pudding. It is good served warm, but also makes wonderful picnic food. Bake it in the morning and take it, in its dish, with your other picnic food. It can then be cut into slices and served cold, as a splendid finale to a (very possibly chilly) happy picnic.

ADVANCE PREPARATION

The dressing for the salad can be made earlier on the day, though the cheese should be grilled just before serving. The olive paste can be made some days before; the beans can be cooked in advance and reheated. The clafoutis is best eaten on the day it is made.

WINE SUGGESTIONS

If you wish, start with Sancerre: its tangy, gooseberry flavour is suited to the goat's cheese. Dolcetto is recommended with the rabbit and the bramble clafoutis, and it can easily be served for the whole meal.

Warm Goat's Cheese Salad

4 individual goat's cheeses (such as the fresh
    cheeses from the Isle of Gigha, or crottins)
walnut oil, to brush
a selection of salad leaves such as lamb's lettuce,
    frisée, lollo rosso, oak leaf
50 g/2 oz walnuts, coarsely chopped

FOR THE DRESSING

$\frac{1}{4}$ tsp Dijon mustard
salt, pepper
1 tbsp sherry vinegar
1 tbsp groundnut oil
3 tbsp walnut oil

1. If you are using cheeses you have marinated in oil, then simply set them on a grill-proof dish. If you are using mature ones with a rind, then carefully remove and discard the rind and brush all over with walnut oil. Place on a grill-proof dish. (If they are very thick, halve them horizontally; they should be about 2 cm/$\frac{3}{4}$ inch thick). Preheat the grill to high.

2. Place the salad leaves in a large bowl. Whisk together the mustard with salt, pepper and the vinegar. Gradually whisk in the oils, to form an emulsion. Pour over the salad and toss well. Add the chopped walnuts. Divide the salad between 4 cold serving plates.

3. Grill the cheeses for about 2–3 minutes (depending on thickness) or until just starting to melt. Do not let them grill too long or they will disappear into a cheesey puddle!

4. Quickly place the cheese on top of the salad and walnuts and serve at once.

DO NOT FREEZE ANY OF THE STARTER

Rabbit with Black Olive Paste

FOR THE PASTE

75 g/3 oz large black olives, stoned (weight after
  stoning)
2 garlic cloves, peeled, crushed
50 g/2 oz anchovy fillets, drained
2 tbsp capers, drained
2 large basil leaves
$\frac{1}{2}$ tsp Dijon mustard
2–3 tsp lemon juice
1 tsp Cognac
black pepper
125 ml/4 fl oz extra virgin olive oil

FOR THE RABBIT

1 tbsp olive oil
125 g/4 oz streaky bacon, diced
1 onion, peeled, chopped
1 leek, sliced
2 tsp plain flour
1 kg/2 lb rabbit joints, cleaned
450 ml/$\frac{3}{4}$ pint dark chicken stock
150 ml/5 fl oz water
2 bay leaves
2 sage leaves
salt, pepper

TO SERVE

2–3 slices of bread (ciabatta is particularly good),
  cut into small rounds, toasted until crispy and
  spread with a little of the olive paste.

SMOKED VENISON WITH MELON

COCONUT AND BANANA CRÊPES

1. To make the paste, place everything except the oil in a food processor and blend together for about a minute. Then add sufficient oil to give a thick paste. Turn into a bowl (or screw-top jar, if making in advance).

2. To cook the rabbit, heat half the oil in a frying pan and gently fry the bacon, onion and leek for 2–3 minutes. Remove to a heavy casserole. Heat the remaining oil in the frying pan while you sprinkle the flour over the rabbit joints. Brown the joints all over for a couple of minutes. (This should be done in batches.) Transfer to the casserole with the vegetables. Preheat the oven to Gas 4/180°C/350°F.

3. Bring the stock and water to the boil, then remove from the heat and add 4–5 tbsp of the black olive paste. Mix well together and pour over the rabbit. Add the bay leaves, sage, salt and pepper. Stir well, cover tightly and cook in the preheated oven until the rabbit is tender, for about 1 hour. Baste a couple of times.

4. Remove from the oven, then skim off (or mop up, using kitchen paper) excess surface oil. Then return to the oven, with the lid off, for about 10 minutes.

5. Check the seasoning and serve at once, garnished with the croutons spread thinly with the paste.

Braised Borlotti Beans

375 g/12 oz dried borlotti beans, soaked overnight
   and drained
2 sticks of celery, whole
2 carrots, peeled, whole
2 large onions, peeled, halved
1 bay leaf
300 ml/10 fl oz chicken stock
300 ml/10 fl oz dry white wine
600 ml/1 pint water
2 tbsp olive oil
black pepper
2 tbsp tomato purée
2 sage leaves
salt

TO SERVE

1 tbsp extra virgin olive oil
1 tbsp freshly chopped parsley

1. Place everything except the salt in a saucepan. Bring to the boil, cover tightly and cook for 2½–3 hours on a very low heat, until the beans are cooked and the liquid absorbed. (Check to see if you require any more liquid.)

2. Remove the celery, carrot, onion and herbs. Season to taste with plenty of salt.

3. To serve, drizzle with the olive oil and sprinkle with the parsley.

THE RABBIT CAN BE FROZEN; THE BEANS ARE BEST NOT FROZEN

Bramble Clafoutis

15 g/½ oz butter
40 g/1½ oz plain flour, sifted
40 g/1½ oz ground almonds
3 eggs
50 g/2 oz caster sugar
15 g/½ oz butter, melted
125 ml/4 fl oz double cream
½ tbsp Kirsch (or blackberry or raspberry
   eau-de-vie)
300 g/10 oz brambles (blackberries)

1. Butter a 20 cm/8 inch flan tin with the 15 g/½ oz butter. Preheat the oven to Gas 5/190°C/375°F.

2. Whizz all the remaining ingredients, except for the brambles, in a food processor (or whisk well together using a balloon whisk) until smooth. Strain if there are any lumps.

3. Place the buttered flan dish into the oven for a couple of minutes, until it becomes very hot. Immediately pour in half of the batter, then carefully place all the brambles on top. Top with the remaining batter.

4. Bake at once in the oven for 30–40 minutes, until it is puffy and golden brown. Serve warm or cold, with or without lightly whipped cream.

THE CLAFOUTIS DOES NOT FREEZE WELL

(Martin Brigdale)

Miller Howe, the well-known lakeside country-house hotel, was opened by JOHN TOVEY in 1971. It is not only his inspirational, unpretentious English food which marks John out as a very well-known and respected chef; he is also a prodigious cookery writer and television personality. Dismissive of food trends and fads, his inimitable style is lighter than it used to be, befitting the five-course dinners served at Miller Howe. He has brought a sense of excitement and distinction to an erstwhile dull approach to English cooking. John very kindly shares a recipe for a salad starter, using salmon.

Trio of Salmon

SERVES 6

375 g/12 oz each of fresh salmon, smoked salmon
    and gravadlax
dry white wine
1 tbsp olive oil
half an iceberg lettuce, shredded

TO GARNISH

lemon slices
salmon eggs
sprigs of parsley
mixed salad leaves

1. Place a baking tray on your hob. Cover the bottom with a mixture of half water and white wine and the olive oil. Bring to the boil, then place the fresh salmon in. Simmer for 2–3 minutes only. Drain and leave to cool.

2. Put the 3 types of salmon decoratively on individual plates: place the cooked salmon on first, then cover it with a mound of iceberg lettuce. Drape the smoked salmon and gravadlax on top.

132

3. Garnish by placing a slice of lemon topped with a spoonful of salmon eggs and a sprig of parsley on top. Arrange the mixed salad leaves decoratively around.

Menu

Smoked Venison with Melon

Herring Gratin
Green Salad with Garlic
Vinaigrette

Tablet and Fruits in Season

Twelve

BOTH THE STARTER AND THE MAIN COURSE IN THIS MENU ARE ADAPTATIONS of classic dishes, changed to suit British ingredients. Instead of the simple Italian dish of prosciutto with melon, I like to use cold-smoked venison with melon and some shavings of parmesan. The famous Swedish dish, Jansson's Temptation, is a luscious creamy concoction of potatoes layered with anchovies. I have used another oily fish – herring – to create this delicious dish. When is a dessert not really a dessert? When it is summer time and all you have to do is prepare a mound of fresh fruit for everyone to pick and choose themselves. Fructose is not sufficient, however, to assuage my embarrassingly sweet tooth: some home-made tablet is the perfect supplement.

Cold-smoked venison makes a delightful change to the more familiar antipasto, prosciutto, which is often served with melon or fresh figs. Nichola and John Fletcher of Auchtermuchty produce the finest smoked venison, by soaking haunches in a brine made of beer, fresh root ginger, salt, pepper sugar and juniper, and then smoking them over hickory chips. It can be eaten simply with wholemeal or rye bread and butter, with freshly cooked asparagus, or stirred into lightly cooked scrambled egg, as you might with smoked salmon. The wafer-thin slices of robust-flavoured meat marry perfectly with sweet, scented melon. Choose either an aromatic Canteloupe, a fragrant juicy Charentais or a Galia, which is a hybrid of Canteloupe and Ogen melons. Top with some shavings of Parmigiano reggiano, with its strong, distinctive flavour. To 'shave' parmesan cheese, either pare the cheese with a very sharp knife or use a vegetable peeler. I never throw away the thick rind from the block of parmesan: throw it into vegetable soups for a deeper flavour, then remove just before serving.

Jansson's Temptation, the Scandinavian dish of potatoes layered with anchovies, cream and onions, is quite delicious. It is reminiscent of the most creamy gratin dauphinois, with some salty anchovies thrown in for added flavour. Since herring is not only easily available from British fishmongers, but also very cheap, it is the ideal substitute for anchovies, which can be too salty for some people's palates. My Finnish friends make a similar dish using fresh or smoked salmon and often add smoked streaky bacon. To make the dish authentically, the potatoes should be cut into matchsticks, so they resemble thin chips. I prefer the thin round slices found in a dauphinois or gratin. It is an ideal dish for the cook to relax completely, as it can linger happily in the oven, covered with foil if necessary, until you are ready. All you need is a crisp green salad to balance the creamy, fishy dish. I adore a predominantly garlicky dressing, but I do appreciate its antisocial qualities. Remember that by roasting the garlic cloves, however, the garlic is rendered milder and sweeter.

As a child, I often attended local fairs and fêtes, where home-baking, jams and sweets were a speciality. The mark of a good fair was if the cake and candy stall had queues miles long, even before the official opening. The first item to sell out was invariably the home-made tablet. Plain vanilla tablet (which has the consistency of a slightly hard fudge, but the flavour of buttery toffee) is not difficult to make, but it should not be attempted if you are likely to be interrupted. The timing is fairly crucial: once the 'soft ball' stage has been reached, it should be removed with great haste and beaten madly. At this stage, you have to know when to stop and pour into the tin. You must catch it just before it becomes grainy, but once it has been sufficiently beaten, to ensure that it sets. Once you have mastered the technique, you can beat in other flavours such as grated white chocolate, ginger syrup or coconut. Serve a large platter of whatever fruit is in season, with the tablet. In midsummer, mounds of either strawberries, redcurrants or raspberries look impressive; they are also everyone's favourite. Offer a sugar sprinkler and whipped cream, for dipping. At the end of the summer or the beginning of the autumn, a dish of wild brambles (blackberries) will be a source of pride, once you have recovered from all the thorn scratches!

ADVANCE PREPARATION

The starter can be prepared and covered with clingfilm an hour before it is to be eaten. It should be dressed with the oil and lemon only at the last minute. The herring dish takes a long time to cook, and can happily wait in the oven or even be reheated. The tablet can be made the day before and kept in an airtight tin.

WINE SUGGESTIONS

Frascati is dry and sharp enough to be served as a suitable alternative to Fino sherry before the meal, and it is suited to the first two courses. In complete contrast, serve Asti Spumante with the tablet and fruit.

Smoked Venison with Melon

125–175 g/4–6 oz wafer-thin slices of cold-smoked
   venison
1 ripe Galia, Canteloupe or Charentais melon
the juice of half a lemon
1–1½ tbsp extra virgin olive oil
25 g/1 oz shavings of Parmigiano reggiano
   (parmesan cheese)

TO SERVE

crusty bread

1. Arrange the venison slices on one side of each of 4 plates.

2. Cut the melon in half, then scoop out the seeds. Peel and slice the flesh into wedges. Lay these on the other half of the plates.

3. Squeeze the lemon juice over the melon, then drizzle a little oil over the venison.

4. Top with shavings of parmesan cheese. Offer crusty French or Italian bread separately.

NONE OF THE STARTER CAN BE FROZEN

Herring Gratin

1.05 kg/2¼ lb large potatoes
15 g/½ oz butter
1 onion, peeled, very finely chopped
1 garlic clove, peeled, crushed
6–8 herring fillets, skinned (about 50 g/2 oz each)
600 ml/1 pint single cream
4 tsp Dijon mustard
salt, freshly ground pepper
25 g/1 oz fresh breadcrumbs
1 tbsp olive oil

1. Peel the potatoes, and cut them into very thin slices using a very sharp knife, a mandoline or the slicing blade on the food processor. Preheat the oven to Gas 6/200°C/400°F.

2. Melt the butter in a frying pan, then fry the onion and garlic gently for 2–3 minutes.

3. Butter a 2.25 litre/4 pint shallow ovenproof dish, then place half the potatoes in the base. Seasoning as you go, continue with a layer of herring (try not to overlap them), then the remaining potatoes.

4. Mix the cream with the mustard and pour over the dish, ensuring all the potatoes are covered.

5. Remove the dish to the middle of the preheated oven and bake for 40 minutes, well covered with buttered foil.

6. Remove the foil, sprinkle over the breadcrumbs and drizzle the oil over the top. Continue to bake, uncovered, for a further 30–40 minutes, or until browned and the potatoes are tender.

7. Remove from the oven, let it rest for at least 5 minutes, then serve in large spoonfuls on warmed plates.

Green Salad with Garlic Vinaigrette

a selection of washed salad leaves, such as lamb'
lettuce, lollo rosso, oakleaf lettuce and watercress

FOR THE VINAIGRETTE

3 large garlic cloves
1 tsp olive oil
1 tbsp red wine vinegar
3–4 tbsp extra virgin olive oil
salt, pepper

1. Preheat the oven to Gas 4/180°C/350°F. Place the salad leaves in a large salad bowl.

2. Remove only the fine outer casing from the cloves of garlic; do not peel them. Place them in a baking dish with 1 tsp olive oil and toss well to coat.

3. Roast them in the preheated oven until they are tender (about 20 minutes), turning once.

4. Once they are cool enough to handle, squeeze out the pulp into a food processor. Add the vinegar and oil, then process until smooth. Add salt and pepper to taste, then push through a sieve.

5. Pour the dressing over the salad leaves and toss well just before serving.

NONE OF THE MAIN COURSE SHOULD BE FROZEN

Tablet

SERVES 10–12

125 g/4 oz unsalted butter
1 kg/2 lb granulated sugar
300 ml/10 fl oz milk
a pinch of salt
1 small tin of condensed milk (200 g/7oz)
1 tsp pure vanilla essence

1. In a heavy-based large saucepan, melt the butter. Add the sugar, milk and salt, stirring until the sugar has dissolved, then slowly bring to the boil. Simmer for 10 minutes, on a fairly high heat.

2. Add the condensed milk, then simmer for a further 8–10 minutes, on a slightly lower heat (so it bubbles, but not fiercely.) Stir constantly.

3. Remove from the heat. Using a hand-held electric beater, beat the mixture for 3–5 minutes (or 10 minutes, by hand) or until the 'soft ball' stage. (Drop a little of the mixture into a cup of very cold water. If it forms a soft ball, it is ready.) If you feel it becoming 'grainy', stop at once: it is ready.

4. Stir in the vanilla essence, then pour the mixture into a buttered swiss roll tin (23 × 33 cm/9 × 13 inches). Allow it to become cold, then cut into small squares and serve with fresh fruit.

THE TABLET FREEZES VERY WELL

The high media profile of ALASTAIR LITTLE exists not merely because he is chef-proprietor of his highly-acclaimed eponymous London restaurant. It is also his eclectic style, evolved from the freedom inherent in so many modern self-taught cooks, which makes people take notice. A Lancastrian by birth, he read archaeology at Cambridge, then began working initially as a waiter, then as a chef in several restaurant kitchens. With his Danish wife, Kirsten, and a third partner, he opened the Soho restaurant in 1985. His cosmopolitan tastes are reflected in the individual and fresh approach he has to cooking. His herring recipe is an example of this uninhibited style.

(Anthony Blake Photography)

Grilled and Marinated Herring

4 herring, filleted (opened out, like a boneless
   kipper)
milk or beaten egg, to dip the herring
fine oatmeal, to coat the herring
150 ml/5 fl oz best quality white wine vinegar (or
   rice vinegar)
2 tbsp sugar
1 onion, cut into rings
1 bay leaf (lime leaf is even better, if you can
   obtain them)
sunflower oil, to fry

1. Place the onion, vinegar, sugar and bay leaf in a saucepan and cook for 20 minutes.

2. Add salt and pepper and let it cool.

3. Dip the herring into the milk or egg, then press them into the oatmeal. Very carefully – and over a gentle heat – fry the fish in the oil, until they are just done (about 2–3 minutes on each side).

4. Lay the herring fillets in a large shallow pottery dish. Pour the marinade over and leave to cool overnight.

5. Serve at room temperature.

Thirteen

THERE ARE INGREDIENTS IN THIS MENU USED IN RATHER UNUSUAL WAYS. The scallops, instead of being either poached or seared, are in fact simply marinated in lime juice and then tossed into a refreshing salad mixture. The scallops do not taste raw, as the citrus juices more or less 'cook' the fish. The main course is full of robust flavours: pork is cooked in a casserole and then topped with something found more commonly on a Sunday breakfast plate – black pudding. It is really an extension of the Lancashire Hotpot, using pork instead of lamb. The crêpes in the pudding contain coconut milk in the batter, so the coconut flavour is subtle; teamed with oven-baked bananas, this is a tropical-inspired dessert – a far cry from the Hotpots of the North!

For the ceviche, it is essential to buy only extremely fresh scallops; frozen ones will definitely not do. Although scallops can be expensive, you need only a few, as it is all mixed with avocado, tomatoes, spring onions and coriander. I like to serve it with warm slices of focaccia or, if you want to be authentic, serve tortilla chips, as the dish is Mexican in origin. Cod, haddock or any chunky white fish can be used, as long as it is very fresh – supermarket pre-packs will not suffice. Lemon juice can also be used in the marinade, but it is slightly weaker than lime juice; increase the time of marinating by about 10–20 minutes. Many people do not like the soft texture of scallop corals (the orange-coloured roe sack), so you can separate these from the white firmer flesh with a sharp knife, before slicing into the lime juice. Scallops are at their best during the winter months, so they make a light refreshing starter for the heavier main course, which is guaranteed to keep out winter chills!

The first time I really enjoyed black pudding was, needless to say, in France, where *boudin* was fried with lightly cooked and buttered apples. The classic combination of pig with apple is manifest in this country in roast pork with apple sauce, but it is easy to forget that black pudding is, after all, pig's blood, and it too marries well with the sweet flavour of apples. I have, therefore, added apples and pears to the pork in the casserole. Incidentally,

Menu

Scallop Ceviche

Pork with Black Pudding Crust
Mashed Potato with Garlic

Coconut and Banana Crêpes

although haggis is made from sheep's pluck (not pig's), it also goes very well with apples, either stewed or in a sauce. Pork can taste rather bland, as it usually comes from intensively reared animals. Nowadays, 'traditional' or free-range pork is, thankfully, to be found more and more, even in supermarkets, and this meat is more succulent and full of flavour. It is usually cheaper to buy a piece of shoulder and cut it yourself, rather than buying it already chopped up. Try to buy the best black pudding available; it should be well seasoned and not too greasy. As a student in Dundee, a late-night snack was occasionally either black or white pudding (oatmeal, mixed with suet and onions) deep-fried in batter, with chips – from a shop called Greasy Pete's. Happily my tastes have changed over the years! The topping of black pudding in the pork recipe forms a tasty crust which provides a contrast of colour and texture. The mashed potato accompaniment is flavoured with garlic and is reminiscent (with its creamy smoothness) of purées my French friends used to feed their babies . . . lucky things!

The coconut crêpes should be fairly thick – not as dainty as a lacy French crêpe. These are then rolled round bananas which are baked in the oven with orange juice, rum and extra coconut. A hot sauce of jaggery (made from palm sugar) and coconut milk, is drizzled over just before serving. Jaggery can be sought from specialist Indian food shops; if you cannot find any, substitute soft brown muscovado sugar instead.

ADVANCE PREPARATION

The ceviche should only be made shortly before serving, or the texture of the scallop will be impaired. The pork casserole can be cooked up to the end of stage 6, and reheated, before topping with the black pudding crust. The coconut crêpes can be made in advance, layered between greaseproof paper and reheated in a low oven. Fill with the banana at the last minute.

WINE SUGGESTIONS

Lindemann Bin 65 Chardonnay, or another Australian or New Zealand Chardonnay, makes an attractive accompaniment to the scallops. With the pork and black pudding serve a Rioja. For the pudding try an Australian Liqueur Muscat which has sufficient sweetness to balance that of the crêpes.

Scallop Ceviche

250 g/8 oz fresh scallops (about 4–5)
the juice of 1 large lime (about 1½–2 tbsp)
2–3 tomatoes, peeled, diced
2 spring onions, finely chopped
1 ripe avocado, peeled, diced
1 heaped tbsp freshly chopped coriander
1 tbsp extra virgin olive oil
salt, pepper

TO SERVE

round lettuce leaves
slivers of ripe avocado
fresh coriander leaves

1. Slice the scallops thinly (into about 3–4 slices) and place them in a glass or ceramic bowl. Add the lime juice, carefully stir to coat every slice, then leave to marinate for 20–25 minutes, stirring gently twice.

2. Combine the tomatoes, spring onions, avocado and coriander with the oil and season to taste with salt and pepper.

3. Drain the scallops of most of their liquid, then carefully toss them into the tomato and avocado mixture. (Be careful you do not break the scallop slices up.)

4. Serve on a bed of round lettuce, decorated with slivers of avocado and coriander. Offer either tortilla chips or warm focaccia.

DO NOT FREEZE

Pork with Black Pudding Crust

1 tbsp olive oil

15 g/½ oz butter

3 tsp quince jelly (apple jelly will also do)

750 g/1½ lb pork shoulder, trimmed, cut into pieces

1 onion, peeled, finely chopped

1 medium leek, finely sliced

2 garlic cloves, peeled, crushed

1 bay leaf

2 sprigs of rosemary

150 ml/5 fl oz dry cider

150 ml/5 fl oz well-flavoured stock (pork, chicken
   or veal)

1 cooking apple (about 250 g/8 oz before peeling),
   peeled, diced

1 pear or 1 quince (about 250 g/8 oz before
   peeling), peeled, diced

salt, pepper

175 g/6 oz black pudding, thinly sliced

15 g/½ oz butter, diced

1. Preheat the oven to Gas 3/160°C/325°F.

2. Heat the oil, butter and 2 tsp of the quince jelly in a casserole. Brown the
    pork on all sides.

3. Remove the pork with a slotted spoon, then fry the onion, leek and garlic
    until softened.

4. Return the meat to the casserole, then add the bay leaf, rosemary, cider,
    stock, apple, pear (quince), salt and pepper. Bring to the boil, then cover
    and remove to the oven for 40 minutes.

5. Remove from the oven and increase the heat to Gas 4/180°C/350°F.

6. With a deep ladle, remove about 150 ml/5 fl oz of the liquid (about 2 ladlefuls) and pour into a small saucepan. Add the remaining quince jelly, then bring this to the boil and simmer for about 5 minutes, until reduced and thickened. Pour this back into the casserole and stir well. Season to taste.

7. Place the black pudding slices on top, overlapping slightly, and dot with butter. Bake in the oven for 25–35 minutes, until the top is crusty. Serve at once.

Mashed Potato with Garlic

750 g/1½ lb potatoes, peeled, quartered
4 garlic cloves, peeled
1 tbsp olive oil
50 g/2 oz butter, softened
125–150 ml/4–5 fl oz hot milk
salt, pepper

1. Place the potatoes and garlic cloves into a large saucepan with the olive oil. Add sufficient water to barely cover, then bring to the boil and simmer for about 15 minutes, until the potatoes are tender.

2. Drain well, then push the potatoes and garlic through a mouli-légume into a warmed bowl.

3. Mix in the butter and sufficient hot milk to make a smooth, creamy purée. Season to taste with salt and pepper.

THE PORK DISH CAN BE FROZEN WITHOUT THE BLACK PUDDING CRUST. THE POTATOES CANNOT BE FROZEN

Coconut and Banana Crêpes

FOR THE CRÊPES

125 g/4 oz plain flour, sifted with a pinch of salt
1 egg
150 ml/5 fl oz milk
150 ml/5 fl oz coconut milk (do not use the watery
    liquid of a coconut; use a tin of coconut milk – it
    has the consistency of thick cream)
butter or oil, to fry

FOR THE FILLING

4 bananas
4 tbsp fresh orange juice
1 tbsp rum
25 g/1 oz soft brown sugar
50 g/2 oz desiccated coconut
15 g/$\frac{1}{2}$ oz butter

FOR THE SAUCE

125 g/4 oz jaggery (or soft brown muscovado
    sugar)
1 tbsp coconut milk

1. For the crêpes, mix everything except the butter or oil in a food
   processor, then strain into a bowl, cover and rest in the fridge for 1 hour.
   (The batter will have the consistency of double cream.)

2. Stir the batter, then rub the hot crêpe pan with kitchen paper dipped
   into the butter or oil. Pour in a little of the batter and make the crêpes.
   The mixture will make about 8 (about 15 cm/6 inches diameter). Stack
   these on a plate, cover with foil and keep them warm in a low oven.

3. For the bananas, preheat the oven to Gas 5/190°C/375°F. Peel the bananas and cut them in half lengthways, then into quarters; place in a buttered baking dish. Mix the orange juice with the rum and pour over the bananas. Mix the coconut with the sugar and sprinkle over the top.

4. Dot with the butter and bake in the oven for about 30 minutes.

5. For the sauce, melt down the jaggery in the milk over a low heat, then bring to the boil and simmer for about 3–4 minutes until you have a sauce-like consistency.

6. To serve, place a crêpe on a plate, then place 2 pieces of banana with some of the juices on top. Roll the crêpe round the banana, then drizzle some of the sauce over the top. Serve at once.

THE UNFILLED CRÊPES CAN BE FROZEN, DEFROSTED AND REHEATED, THEN FILLED WITH THE BANANAS.

Since PAUL HEATHCOTE opened his own restaurant in his native Lancashire in 1990, it has been widely recognised as one of the best in the North of England. The experience of having worked at Sharrow Bay Hotel, the Connaught and Le Manoir aux Quat' Saisons, has imbued in Paul's imaginative cooking solid classical roots. He cooks passionately with local produce, supplemented with the best quality ingredients from around the country. His recipe for Black Pudding – a Lancashire speciality – elevates this everyday dish to the realms of *haute cuisine*.

Black Pudding

1 black pudding skin (stick size)
600 ml/1 pint pig's blood
¼ onion, chopped and boiled until soft
50 g/2 oz oats
1 sprig of rosemary
1 sprig of thyme
1 bay leaf, crushed
50 g/2 oz sultanas
75 ml/3 fl oz white wine vinegar
500 g/1 lb veal or lamb's sweetbread
olive oil
175 g/6 oz cooked foie gras
salt, pepper

1. Soak the sultanas in the vinegar until all of it has been soaked up.

2. Place in a pan over a low heat until most of the vinegar has evaporated. Do not allow it to caramelise.

3. Blanch the sweetbreads into boiling water for 1 minute, then remove from the water and peel off the outside membrane.

4. Cut them into large dice and fry off in olive oil until golden brown. Reserve to one side.

5. Cut the foie gras into dice and mix with the sweetbread.

6. Warm the blood over a bain-marie until it starts to thicken, stirring continually. Pass through a sieve to remove any white membrane.

7. Crush the bay leaf and remove the rosemary and thyme from their stalks. Add these to the sweetbreads and foie gras, with the blood, oats, sultanas and onion. Season with salt and pepper.

8. Place into the pudding skin and poach in a bain-marie in a moderate oven (Gas 3–4/160–180°C/325–350°F) until the pudding is just cooked (about 40–45 minutes).

9. Cool the pudding, then slice, brush with olive oil and grill. Serve hot, straight from the grill.

Menu

Tomato with Pesto Spaghetti

Scallop and Langoustine Stew
Lemon Barley

Rhubarb and Pernod Ice-Cream

Fourteen

THERE ARE SOME OF MY FAVOURITE TASTES AND TEXTURES IN THIS MENU. I adore any dish made with fresh basil, and a home-made pesto sauce takes some beating. The starter is a mound of pesto-flavoured spaghetti on tomato, with some melting cheese over the top. The main course incorporates the succulent firm texture of scallops with juicy, meaty langoustines. They are poached in a mixture of fish stock and vegetables, enhanced at the end by cream, tomatoes and basil. The ice-cream will not be everyone's favourite. The aniseed flavour of Pernod is an acquired taste; one which many have no intention of acquiring! You can reduce the amount of Pernod you add, according to your guests' preferences.

I make as much pesto sauce as possible each summer, when fresh basil is inexpensive. It freezes very well, or can be kept in the fridge for about six weeks. Purée a large bunch of basil leaves with 1 crushed garlic clove, $\frac{1}{2}$ tsp salt, 2 tbsp freshly grated parmesan and 2 tbsp pine nuts. Add about 125 ml/4 fl oz extra virgin olive oil, to form a thickish paste. Apart from adding pesto to pasta, it livens up vinaigrettes, hot garlic bread, savoury flans, thick vegetables soups or ratatouilles. Basil is a handy plant to have on the kitchen window-sill during the winter; it can also be grown from seed in a sunny sheltered spot in the garden, once any danger of frost is over. It has a great affinity with Mediterranean vegetables such as tomatoes, peppers, aubergines and courgettes, and is always best shredded into a dish towards the end of cooking, to retain its bright green colour and sweet, almost clove-like taste. In this recipe, a twirl of freshly cooked spaghetti is mixed with some pesto and ricotta cheese, then placed on a slice of tomato (it is important to have tomatoes with plenty of flavour, not the bland greenhouse variety), topped with a slice of melting cheese, then baked in the oven. It definitely falls into the category of an amusing little starter!

The scallops I use for the seafood stew are Great Scallops, whose shells are about 13–15 cm/5–6 inches in diameter. If you are using Queen Scallops (whose shell is about half the size), then increase the number you are cooking. My fishmonger obtains his scallops from the waters around

155

Orkney and Shetland, or from the west coast of Scotland. He often smokes them with Italian herbs, for an unusual starter, with brown bread and butter. The langoustines (also known as Dublin Bay prawns or Scampi) in the stew need to be beheaded and shelled before cooking. As they are live, you may want to ask your fishmonger to carry out the execution, if you are squeamish. It is in fact very easy: you twist the tail off the body, then crack the shell with your fingers. By tightly gripping the middle section of the tail, you should be able to pull out the whole intestinal tract (which is like a black thread). You then complete the shelling process. The heads can be used to flavour the fish stock, in which you then poach the tails and the scallops. I think barley, flavoured with lemon, is perfect to mop up the tasty juices in the stew, which I recommend serving in wide soup bowls rather than on plates.

Rhubarb and custard for school dinners has done nothing to endear this vegetable (for so it is technically classified) to the average British palate. Young, tender stalks of rhubarb, however, have a variety of uses: it makes a delicious chutney, flavoured with either orange or ginger; combined with some apricots and almonds, rhubarb jam is a treat for a tea-time scone or crumpet; and, baked with a vanilla pod or cinnamon stick, it is good cold, for breakfast, with some thick yoghurt. I first tasted rhubarb with Pernod in a freshly made chocolate truffle, at a London restaurant: I thought the combination quite sublime. If you have any sweet cicely, add some finely chopped leaves to the ice-cream, as its sweet anise flavour enhances the aniseed-tasting Pernod. Sweet cicely can also be used with gooseberries, redcurrants or pears.

ADVANCE PREPARATION

The starter cannot be made in advance. The seafood can be cleaned and shelled before, but should be freshly cooked. The barley can be reheated, but some extra liquid may need to be added. The rhubarb ice-cream is best eaten on the day it is made.

WINE SUGGESTIONS

Try Californian Fumé Blanc with this meal. Alternatively, start with Fino Sherry and continue with your favourite New World Chardonnay. It will be difficult for any wine to complement or compete with the aniseed flavour of the Pernod in the pudding: therefore let the pudding be consumed without wine and round off the meal with port or brandy.

Tomato with Pesto Spaghetti

FOR THE SPAGHETTI

250 g/8 oz dried spaghetti
2 tbsp pesto sauce
200 g/7 oz ricotta
black pepper
1 heaped tbsp freshly grated parmesan
4 thin slices of mozzarella or fontina cheese

FOR THE TOMATO

2 large firm tomatoes
$\frac{1}{2}$ tsp caster sugar
1 tbsp extra virgin olive oil

TO SERVE

extra virgin olive oil

1. Preheat the oven to Gas 2/150°C/300°F. Cut the tomatoes into 2 slices each, giving you 4 × 1 cm/$\frac{1}{2}$ inch slices. Place these on an oiled baking tray, sprinkle with the sugar, then drizzle over the oil. Bake in the oven for about half an hour, until the tomatoes are just tender. Increase the oven to Gas 6/200°C/400°F.

2. Cook the spaghetti until slightly undercooked, then drain well. Mix the pesto, ricotta, pepper and parmesan together, then stir this into the spaghetti. (The mixture will be fairly stiff.)

157

3. Using a fork and large spoon, twirl a quarter of it into a coil-shape and arrange this carefully on to the tomato. Top with the slice of mozzarella or fontina. Repeat with the others, then bake in the oven for about 10–12 minutes until the cheese is melted.

4. To serve, use a fish-slice to slide the tomato layer on to a serving plate, then drizzle with some of the oil and serve at once.

ONLY THE PESTO SAUCE CAN BE FROZEN

Scallop and Langoustine Stew

12 live langoustines
750 ml/1¼ pints fish stock
2 tbsp Noilly Prat
8–12 fresh scallops, (about 750 g/1½lb) cleaned
1 tbsp olive oil
4 shallots, peeled, finely chopped
1 fennel bulb, outer leaves removed, finely
    chopped
1 leek, finely chopped
4 tomatoes (or 2 large ones), peeled, diced
6–8 basil leaves, shredded
150 ml/5 fl oz double cream
salt, freshly ground pepper

TO SERVE

basil sprigs

1. Remove the heads from the langoustines (or get your fishmonger to do so) and wash them. Wash the tails, remove the intestinal thread and very carefully shell them. Take care not to tear the delicate flesh of the langoustines.

2. Place the heads (with their claws) in a large saucepan with the fish stock and the Noilly Prat. Bring the liquid to the boil, then simmer very gently for 20 minutes. Sieve into a bowl and discard the langoustine heads.

3. If the scallops are very large, cut in two, horizontally.

4. Heat the oil in a large heavy-based pan. Fry the shallots gently for 1 minute, then add the fennel and leek. Fry gently for 3–4 minutes, then add the strained fish stock. Bring this to the boil, then reduce (over a fairly high heat) for about 10 minutes, until the liquid is reduced to about half.

5. Lower the heat to a very gentle simmer and add the scallops. Poach for 1 minute. Then add the langoustines and poach for a further 1 minute.

6. Remove the scallops and langoustines with a slotted spoon to a bowl.

7. Add the tomatoes, basil and cream and bring to the boil. Reduced the liquid for about 5 minutes, until just becoming thick, then season to taste with salt and pepper.

8. Return the scallops and langoustines to the pan and very gently reheat for about 1 minute. Serve at once in warmed bowls, and garnish with a sprig of basil.

Lemon Barley

200 g/7 oz pearl barley
300 ml/10 fl oz water
½ tsp salt
the juice and grated zest of 1 large lemon
2 tbsp freshly chopped parsley
1 tbsp extra virgin olive oil

1. Preheat the oven to Gas 3/160°C/325°F. In a casserole, combine the barley, water, salt and lemon juice and zest. Bring to the boil, stir well, then cover tightly and place in the oven.

2. Cook for about 30–40 minutes, stirring once, until all the liquid is absorbed and the barley tender.

3. Remove from the heat, stir in the parsley and olive oil and serve at once, with the stew.

NONE OF THE MAIN COURSE CAN BE FROZEN

SALMON AND SORREL SOUP

RHUBARB AND PERNOD ICE-CREAM

Rhubarb and Pernod Ice-Cream

375 g/12 oz rhubarb, trimmed, washed, cut into 5
  cm/2 inch pieces
25 g/1 oz caster sugar
the grated zest and juice of 1 small orange
3 tsp Pernod
300 ml/10 fl oz double cream
25 g/1 oz icing sugar, sifted
finely chopped sweet cicely leaves, optional

TO SERVE

sweet cicely leaves, to garnish

1. Place the rhubarb, caster sugar, orange zest and juice in a saucepan.
   Bring to the boil slowly, then simmer for a few minutes until the rhubarb
   is just tender.

2. Purée or mash well, then place in a bowl. Stir in the Pernod, once it has
   cooled. Allow to become quite cold.

3. Whip the icing sugar and cream until it is floppy, then carefully fold the
   rhubarb, sweet cicely and Pernod into the cream.

4. Pour this into an ice-cream machine to churn until it is set. (Or freeze in
   a bowl, beating every half hour.)

5. To serve, remove from the freezer 10 minutes before serving. Garnish
   with sweet cicely.

Chef **BRIAN TURNER** is another of Britain's culinary success stories. As a schoolboy, he helped his father cook in his transport café near Leeds. He then progressed to the kitchens of London's Simpsons in The Strand, The Savoy Grill, then Beau Rivage Palace, Switzerland. Spells at Claridges and The Capital Hotel preceded the opening in 1986 of his own restaurant in Knightsbridge. The importance of treating the finest ingredients with simplicity and reverence underlies his unpretentious, confident style of cooking. Brian's sumptuous dish of scallops with garlic, tomatoes and artichokes is one of his personal favourites; it is also remarkably simple to produce at home.

Layered Scallops with Garlic, Tomatoes and Artichokes in Champagne Butter Sauce

12 scallops
12 cooked artichoke hearts
12 tomatoes concassé
olive oil
4 chopped shallots
1 garlic clove

FOR THE SAUCE

half a glass champagne
2 chopped shallots
125 ml/4 fl oz white wine
1 tbsp white wine vinegar
175 g/6 oz unsalted butter
crushed peppercorns
150 ml/5 fl oz double cream
dill
chopped chives

1. Heat a little olive oil and add the crushed garlic and chopped shallots. Add the diced tomato skins and sprinkle with seasoning.

2. Remove from the heat. Thinly slice the scallops, clean the artichoke hearts and slice into eight pieces.

3. Arrange the scallops in 4 rings, then place on top a layer of tomatoes, followed by a layer of artichokes. Repeat the layering until all of your ingredients are used.

4. Sprinkle with a little olive oil and steam for about 6 minutes. Be careful not to overcook.

5. For the sauce, pour the champagne, white wine and the vinegar into a saucepan. Add the chopped shallots and peppercorns and simmer until the alcohol has reduced.

6. Add the double cream, then add the butter, and stir until the sauce thickens slightly.

7. Season with chopped dill and stir well. Sprinkle with chives and serve at once: carefully demould the rings of scallops on to 4 warmed plates and spoon some of the sauce around.

Menu

Salmon and Sorrel Soup

Duck with Gooseberries
Potatoes with Thyme in a Paper Parcel

Warm Bitter Chocolate Cake

Fifteen

THE COLOURS IN THIS MENU ARE BRIGHT AND APPEALING. THE SOUP IS salmon pink, with shades of bright green from the sorrel pesto. The crisp golden duck is sauced with a paler green gooseberry purée, accompanied by rich, russet-coloured beans. The dessert is a dark bitter chocolate, which is dredged in white icing sugar to add to its visual impact.

There are many versions of *Kalakeitto* – fish soup – in Finland. Burbot, pike or perch are cooked in chunks with potatoes, peppercorns, dill and a mixture of milk and fish stock. The soup is sometimes preceded by blinis topped with burbot roe, during the season. One memorable lunch I had was in Finnish Lapland, where the fish soup was made with locally caught salmon. Dill featured strongly, to enhance not only the flavour but also the colour. I have adapted a Finnish recipe by adding a sorrel pesto at the end, instead of using dill. The sharp lemony taste of sorrel makes it a perfect partner with salmon. Any leftover pesto keeps well in the fridge and can be tossed into pasta with some freshly grated parmesan cheese.

The combination of sharp green gooseberries (not the sweeter pink dessert variety) with oily fish such as mackerel or herring is well known. They are also good with meats which have a tendency to richness such as goose (although there is apparently no etymological link between the two words) and duck. It is a very easy sauce to cook, as you do not even need to top and tail the gooseberries, since it is all to be sieved at the end. Duck breasts can be found in most supermarkets throughout the year; but look out for wild ducks such as mallard or teal from game-dealers during their season (September to February). Teal is a tiny creature, so should be roasted whole; mallard is a larger bird and, since its flesh is leaner than its fatter domestic relatives, should not be overcooked. My recipe is geared for the readily available English or French domestic duck; if you are cooking wild duck, reduce the cooking time and baste with melted butter or the flesh will dry out.

To accompany the main course, there are tiny potatoes baked in baking parchment, with a thyme-flavoured oil. I make this by putting a handful of fresh thyme into a large jar, topping up with extra virgin olive oil and a dash of white wine vinegar, sealing, then placing on a sunny window-sill for about three weeks, shaking daily. It is then strained into a clean bottle with a fresh sprig of thyme and used to flavour pastas, meats and vegetables. I make the same with rosemary, to brush over warm focaccia. If you do not have thyme oil, use olive oil and fresh thyme sprigs.

The chocolate cake for dessert should be served warm and in small slices. It is very rich and has a texture reminiscent of brownies – fudgey and dense, with a crispy exterior. The chocolate in the recipe should have the highest cocoa solid content possible – 70 per cent is best. I like to use Valrhona's Guanaja Noire. You can serve the cake with a little raspberry ice-cream or just with some pouring cream. Although it is best freshly baked, it lasts well in the fridge for several days, although the texture becomes more solid.

ADVANCE PREPARATION

The soup should be made at the last minute; the sorrel pesto can be made a couple of days in advance. The gooseberry purée can be cooked earlier, but should be added to the sauce while the duck is cooking. The cake is best freshly baked, although you can bake it earlier and reheat gently in a low oven.

WINE SUGGESTIONS

A Californian Chenin Blanc is recommended with the soup and the duck, or good Vouvray. With the chocolate cake try Moscato d'Asti Vigna Senza, a sweet sparkling wine; or, if you prefer something stronger, Muscat de Beaumes de Venise.

Salmon and Sorrel Soup

FOR THE SORREL PESTO

25 g/1 oz fresh parsley leaves
175 g/6 oz fresh young sorrel leaves
2 tbsp pine nuts
2 tbsp freshly grated parmesan cheese
2 garlic cloves, peeled, crushed
$\frac{1}{2}$ tsp salt
1 tsp lemon juice
100–125 ml/$3\frac{1}{2}$–4 fl oz extra virgin olive oil

FOR THE SOUP

4–6 potatoes (about 1 kg/2 lb before peeling),
   peeled, diced
900 ml/$1\frac{1}{2}$ pints fish stock
1 large leek, cleaned, very thinly sliced
8 black peppercorns
500 g/1 lb fresh salmon (I use the tail end of the
   fillet), cut into chunks
salt

1. For the pesto, place the first 7 ingredients in a food processor and process until the leaves are finely chopped. Then slowly add the oil (through the feeder tube, with the machine running), until it has the consistency of a thick paste. Taste for seasoning.

2. For the soup, place the potatoes in a saucepan with the fish stock. Bring to the boil, then simmer for about 10 minutes until the potatoes are just tender.

3. Add the leeks and peppercorns, then place the salmon on top. Cover with a lid and simmer for 10–15 minutes, over a low heat, until the fish is just cooked. Do not stir vigorously, or you will break up the fish.

4. Season to taste with salt, then ladle into warmed soup bowls. Stir in $\frac{1}{2}$ tbsp of the sorrel pesto into each bowl and serve at once. Leave a small bowl of extra pesto if people want to top up their supply.

THE SORREL PESTO FREEZES WELL; DO NOT FREEZE THE SOUP

Duck with Gooseberries

4 boneless duck breasts (about 175 g/6 oz each)
1 tsp honey, melted
375 g/12 oz gooseberries
40 g/1$\frac{1}{2}$ oz caster sugar
150 ml/5 fl oz dry white wine
2–3 shallots, peeled, chopped
150 ml/5 fl oz duck or dark chicken stock
2–3 large fresh sage leaves
salt, pepper

1. Preheat the oven to Gas 7/220°C/425°F. Heat a large heavy-based frying pan until it is very hot, then place in the duck breasts, skin-side down. (You will not need to use fat to cook the duck if the pan is extremely hot.)

2. Brown the breasts, turning once. This should take no more than 3 minutes.

3. Using a slotted spoon, remove the duck to a roasting tin (skin side up) and brush the top with the honey. Roast in the oven for about 15 minutes (they will still be fairly pink; 20 minutes will cook them to medium).

4. Meanwhile, place the gooseberries in a saucepan with the sugar and wine and simmer until they are soft (for about 10–15 minutes), then push them through a sieve.

5. In the frying pan which you used for the duck breasts, heat the residual fat and fry the shallots gently for 2–3 minutes, then add the stock and the sage and bring to the boil. Reduce the liquid to half, then add the gooseberry purée and simmer for a further 5–10 minutes until you have a sauce-like consistency.

6. Season well with salt and pepper, sieve and keep warm until the duck is ready.

7. Remove the duck after the 15–20 minutes, then rest, covered loosely with foil, for 5 minutes. Cut the breasts into slices and place on warmed plates. Add any juices from the roasting tin to the sauce and spoon a little of the sauce around the duck.

Potatoes with Thyme in a Paper Parcel

750 g/1½ lb tiny new or 'baby salad' potatoes (all of
   a uniform size)
25 g/1 oz butter
1 tbsp thyme oil (or olive oil)
3–4 sprigs of fresh thyme
salt

1. Scrub the potatoes well. Preheat the oven to Gas 5/190°C/375°F.

2. Lay 2 large pieces of baking parchment on a baking tray. Place the potatoes on top and sprinkle well with salt. Dot with the butter and drizzle over the oil. Tuck in the thyme.

3. Gather up the edges and fold over to seal the parcel tightly. (Depending on the size of your paper, you may have to overlay 2 large pieces of the parchment crosswise.)

169

4. Bake in the oven for about an hour, depending on the size of the potatoes. You can test with the tip of a sharp knife, through the paper, after 50 minutes.

5. To serve, either cut the paper and tip the contents into a warmed dish or carefully slide the parcel on to a warmed serving plate and open at the table.

NONE OF THE MAIN COURSE CAN BE FROZEN

Warm Bitter Chocolate Cake

SERVES 8–10

300 g/10 oz best bitter chocolate (with very high
    percentage of cocoa solids – preferably 70 per
    cent)
150 g/5 oz unsalted butter
4 eggs, separated
150 g/5 oz caster sugar
40 g/1½ oz plain flour, sifted
a pinch of salt

1. Butter and line the base of a 24 cm/9½ inch loose-bottom cake tin.
   Preheat the oven to Gas 4/180°C/350°F.

2. Melt the chocolate, butter and sugar in a double boiler. Remove from
   the heat, stir well and cool for about 10 minutes.

3. Beat in the egg yolks, one at a time.

4. Whisk the egg whites until they form soft peaks. Fold in the flour, salt
   and a little of the egg-white mixture into the chocolate mixture. Then
   add the remaining egg whites, folding carefully.

5. Pour the mixture into the prepared tin, tap the base on the table to level
   the surface, then bake in the middle of the oven for 35–40 minutes.
   Allow the cake to cook in the tin for about 20 minutes, then carefully
   remove the edges and base of the cake and slide on to the serving plate.
   Dredge with icing sugar. You can serve this either with pouring cream,
   vanilla or raspberry ice-cream.

DO NOT FREEZE THE CAKE

NICK NAIRN is chef-proprietor of Braeval Old Mill, near Aberfoyle in the heart of the Trossachs. Passionate about the use of top-quality ingredients, innovative and skilful in his approach to cooking, it is little wonder that Nick's well-deserved reputation extends all over the country: he was the youngest chef to receive a Michelin star in Scotland. His versatility means he can turn his hand to any dish, from delectable canapé to the finest sweet pastry. Here is one of his favourite recipes, for mallard duck with a game and cassis sauce.

Breast of Mallard Duck with Wild Rice and a Game and Cassis Sauce

2 plump mallard, breasts removed and carcasses
    chopped into 2.5 cm/1 inch pieces
4 tbsp duck fat
150 g/5 oz wild rice, soaked overnight and drained
$\frac{1}{2}$ onion, 1 carrot, $\frac{1}{2}$ stick celery, 4 garlic cloves, all
    cut into 5 mm/$\frac{1}{4}$ inch dice
2 bay leaves
6 crushed peppercorns
2 sprigs of thyme
300 ml/10 fl oz veal jus
300 ml/10 fl oz chicken stock
300 ml/10 fl oz water
125 ml/4 fl oz port
2 tbsp Cassis
1 tsp double cream
15 g/$\frac{1}{2}$ oz cold butter
salt, pepper

1. Preheat the oven to Gas 9/240°C/475°F. Roast the chopped carcasses in a hot oven, until they are browned all over. Heat 2 tbsp duck fat in a saucepan until smoking. Add all the diced onion, carrot, celery and most

of the garlic. Sauté until they are well coloured (about 10–15 minutes). Add 1 bay leaf, the peppercorns, 1 sprig thyme, the roasted duck carcass and stir well, adding the port to deglaze. Reduce the liquid until it is syrupy, then add the jus, the stock, the water and bring to the boil. Simmer for 1 hour.

2. Strain the liquid through a very fine sieve and refrigerate overnight. The next day, skim off the fat and pour the clear liquid (which will be like jelly) into a saucepan, bring to the boil and reduce the liquid to 300 ml/ 10 fl oz.

3. Add the cream, whisk in the butter, add the Cassis and season. Keep warm.

4. For the rice, bring it to the boil with the remaining garlic, 1 bay leaf, 1 sprig of thyme and sufficient water to cover. Season the water well, then simmer for 20–30 minutes until it is tender. Drain and allow it to dry out over a very low heat.

5. For the duck, season the breasts with salt and pepper. Heat the remaining 2 tbsp duck fat in a frying pan (one which you can also use in the oven). Brown the duck breasts all over. Put the pan, with the breasts, into the preheated hot oven for about 5 minutes until they are firm to the touch. Remove and leave them in a warm place for 10 minutes.

6. Pour the juices and the fat from the duck pan into the rice, mix well and check the seasoning. Place a bed of rice on to a warmed plate, slice the breast on top and pour the sauce around. Serve with roasted turnip and stir-fried cabbage and juniper.

Menu

Lamburgers on Pitta Bread

Red Mullet with Fennel
Olive Oil Sauce • Tabbouleh

Macadamia Nut and
White Chocolate Ice-Cream
and Cookies

Sixteen

THERE ARE STRONG FLAVOURS IN THIS MENU: LAMB 'BURGERS' ARE TOPPED with red peppers, capers and olives for an unusual starter; red mullet is grilled simply and served on a bed of fennel with a herby olive oil sauce; tabbouleh, flavoured with lemon juice, parsley and mint, soak up those delicious oily juices; the dessert is an ice-cream with some buttery cookies, both laden with a combination of macadamia nuts and white chocolate.

It is important to use extra lean minced lamb for the burgers; you want no hint of greasiness. They should be well seasoned, as the red pepper topping is mixed with the dominant flavours of capers and black olives. As the burger is turned on the grill, it is topped with a slice of mozzarella, which melts to give a gooey golden crust. The burger is served sitting on a round wholemeal pitta bread, which has been split in half and toasted. 'Mini pittas' are usually round and are therefore the ideal shape; if only ovals are available, then trim to size with a pastry-cutter. You could also serve the burgers on rounds of warmed ciabatta, focaccia or pumpernickel bread.

Red mullet is usually associated with the Mediterranean, but is in fact found around warmer southern English waters in the summer. It tastes fairly strong, almost gamey, and is, therefore, matched admirably by the bold flavour of fennel. Whole red mullet is often stuffed with either slices of fennel bulb or stalks and leaves of the herb fennel, then baked or grilled. If the appearance of a whole fish – with its head and staring eyes – does nothing for you (or if you do not enjoy grappling with the bones), then you can fillet the fish first; but it is better to use larger fish than specified.

Bulb fennel (it is sometimes known as Florence fennel or finocchio) is a variety of the herb fennel which has a swollen edible base. The herb fennel is well known as one of the best herbs to go with fish; either its dried seeds or its feathery green leaves are invariably used in fish stocks and sauces. Bronze fennel is a milder flavoured herb, and is used primarily as decoration. It is also an interesting addition to a salad of mixed greens and herbs, to accompany a fish dish.

Tabbouleh can be made with a variety of ingredients, but the essentials are bulgar (cracked) wheat, parsley, mint, and lots of lemon juice. It makes an ideal accompaniment to hot spicy dishes, or to cold flans, barbecue dishes or roasts. I make a couscous salad with almost the same ingredients, using couscous instead of bulgar and adding extra chopped mint; it is delicious with grilled lamb chops.

The herbs in the olive oil sauce can be altered depending on what you are serving it with. The essential is to use the best extra virgin oil you can afford. Any leftover sauce can be refrigerated and used the next day as a salad dressing, or as a dipping sauce for warm Italian bread.

After these oily flavours, my palate craves a sweet creamy taste, so the combination of rich ice-cream and luscious buttery cookies is ideal . . . but then, as I think you will appreciate by now, I do have a sweet tooth! I first had macadamia nuts in Australia, where they are justifiably proud of what they call Queensland nuts. Australians cover them in milk chocolate, or salt them to go with drinks, or use them in pies, tarts and ices. They taste rich and creamy – almost buttery – and are the perfect partner for white chocolate, which should be the least sweet you can find. The cookies have a crisp exterior and a slightly chewy inner, befitting American-style cookies.

ADVANCE PREPARATION

The lamburgers can be prepared and shaped, then refrigerated for up to 6 hours. The tabbouleh can be made earlier in the day, then brought back to room temperature from the fridge. The olive oil sauce and red mullet need last minute attention. The ice-cream and cookies are better freshly made.

WINE SUGGESTIONS

Hamilton Russel Pinot Noir from South Africa has the body and taste to accompany both the lamburgers and the mullet. If you would prefer to serve a white wine with the mullet try Torres Vina Sol. The nutty sweetness of the pudding can be complemented by either Moscato Spumante, or an Oloroso Sherry.

MACADAMIA NUT AND WHITE CHOCOLATE ICE-CREAM AND COOKIES

GOAT'S CHEESE AND RED PEPPER TART

Lamburgers on Pitta Bread

500 g/1 lb lean minced lamb
25 g/1 oz fresh breadcrumbs
1 medium onion, peeled, finely chopped
2 tbsp freshly chopped mint
1 tsp ground cumin
1 egg, beaten
salt, pepper
4 slices of mozzarella cheese

FOR THE TOPPING

1 red pepper, cut into quarters and deseeded
1 tbsp black olives, stoned, chopped
1 tbsp capers, drained
1 tbsp olive oil
1 tsp sherry vinegar
salt, pepper

TO SERVE

rounds of wholemeal pitta bread, halved and
    toasted

1. Combine the first 7 ingredients together, seasoning well with salt and pepper. Using wet hands, form into 8 small burger shapes. Chill for about an hour.

2. Meanwhile, grill the pepper until charred and black. Wrap tightly in foil for 20 minutes, then remove the skin (it will peel away easily). Cut into slivers, then mix with the olives, capers, oil, vinegar, salt and pepper.

3. Heat the grill to very hot, then grill the burgers for 2–3 minutes on one side. Carefully turn, then grill for a further 2 minutes. Place a slice of cheese on top of each, and grill for 1 minute, until the mozzarella is bubbling and golden.

4. Place the toasted pitta bread on to warmed plates, then slide the burger on top. Spoon some of the red pepper (and a little of the juices) over and serve at once.

THE STARTER CANNOT BE FROZEN

Red Mullet with Fennel

4 red mullet (about 150 g/5 oz each), gutted, scaled
1½ tbsp extra virgin olive oil
2 bulbs of fennel, coarse outer leaves removed, thinly sliced
1 tsp lemon juice
1 tbsp chives or parsley, finely chopped, salt, pepper

1. Slash the mullet on either side with a sharp knife or scissors (to ensure even cooking) and snip off the fins (or they will burn). Preheat the grill to high.

2. Brush with ½ tbsp of the oil and place in grilling pan. Grill for about 4 minutes on each side.

3. Meanwhile, steam the fennel for 10 minutes, then toss it with the lemon juice and remaining oil. Add the chives or parsley, season to taste and spoon into the centre of a warmed plate. Place the fish on top, then surround with the warmed olive oil sauce.

Olive Oil Sauce

the juice of 1 lemon
125m/4 fl oz extra virgin olive oil
1 garlic clove, peeled
1 tomato, peeled, seeded, diced
1 tbsp freshly chopped basil
½ tbsp freshly chopped chives or parsley
salt, pepper

1. Place the lemon juice in a saucepan with the oil and garlic. Add the tomato, salt and pepper. Gently heat until warm, then remove from the heat, cover and allow to infuse for about an hour.

2. Just before serving, reheat slowly until very hot, remove the garlic clove, stir in the herbs, check for seasoning and serve around the fish.

Tabbouleh

450 ml/¾ pint water
2 tbsp freshly squeezed lemon juice
3 tbsp extra virgin olive oil
250 g/8 oz bulgar wheat
4 plum tomatoes (or 2 large tomatoes), peeled,
    seeded, diced
5 tbsp freshly chopped parsley
1 tbsp freshly chopped mint
salt, to taste

1. In a saucepan, bring the water, 1 tbsp lemon juice and 2 tbsp oil to the boil. Pour in the bulgar wheat, stir, then remove from the heat. Cover and leave for 10 minutes.

2. Fluff up the mixture with a fork, then cover again and leave for 20 minutes.

3. Mix in the remaining lemon juice and oil, the tomatoes, parsley, mint and salt to taste. Stir well and serve at room temperature. (You may need extra lemon juice, if you do not think it is sufficiently sharp.)

NONE OF THE MAIN COURSE CAN BE FROZEN

Macadamia Nut and White Chocolate Ice-Cream and Cookies

FOR THE ICE-CREAM

450 ml/¾ pint double cream
150 g/5 oz white chocolate, chopped
2 egg yolks
50 g/2 oz macadamia nuts, halved, toasted

FOR THE COOKIES

125 g/4 oz unsalted butter, at room temperature
125 g/4 oz golden caster sugar
1 large egg, beaten
1 tsp vanilla essence
125 g/4 oz plain flour, sifted
½ tsp baking powder
¼ tsp salt
125 g/4 oz white chocolate chips
125 g/4 oz macadamia nuts, in chunks

1. For the ice-cream, heat the cream in a saucepan with the chocolate. Do not let it boil.

2. Stir until the chocolate is smooth, then remove from the heat. Whisk the egg yolk and very slowly pour some of the hot cream mixture over the yolks, whisking constantly. Return this egg mixture to the saucepan with the remaining cream mixture. Heat everything together, over a very low heat, whisking or stirring constantly, until it thickens slightly. This will take about 4–5 minutes.

3. Cool by placing the saucepan over a bowl of iced water. Stir from time to time, so a skin does not form. Once it is cold, churn in an ice-cream machine (or freeze in a freezer, stirring every half hour). When it is almost frozen, add the nuts, stir well, then freeze until solid. Remove from the freezer 10 minutes before serving, with the cookies.

4. For the cookies, preheat the oven to Gas 5/190°C/375°F. In a food processor, blend the butter, sugar, egg and vanilla together, for about one minute. Add the flour, baking powder and salt and process for about 20 seconds. (It may help to scrape down the sides of the machine.)

5. Add the chocolate and the nuts, by using a 'pulse' button; you must process very briefly, so you do not chop up the nuts and chocolate.

6. Mound dessertspoonfuls on to 2 buttered baking sheets, spacing them well apart. Bake in the preheated oven for about 15 minutes, or until they are light brown at the edges. Cool for 2–3 minutes on the baking sheet, then remove to a wire rack to become cold.

THE COOKIES FREEZE VERY WELL

SHAUN HILL has been cooking at one of the England's most splendid hotels, Gidleigh Park in Devon, since 1985. Prior to his appointment as head chef, he had worked at Robert Carrier's restaurant, The Gay Hussar, The Capital Hotel, and others. Non-conformist in style, Shaun's cooking has won many well-earned awards and culinary honours. His classical training ensures that his imaginative, inventive approach does not result in flavours and ingredients being combined purely for gimmickry. Shaun's much-admired originality is evident in this splendid marriage of flavours: red mullet with celeriac, lemon and olive oil.

Red Mullet with Celeriac, Lemon and Olive Oil

4 × 300 g/10 oz red mullet
1 kg/2 lb celeriac
125 g/4 oz crème fraîche
2 lemons
75 ml/3 fl oz extra virgin olive oil (preferably
    Italian or French)
a little groundnut oil, to fry
salt, pepper

1. For the mullet, scale the fish by scraping from head to tail with a sharp knife. Fillet the fish by cutting along the line of its backbone toward the belly. If you do it carefully you will have 2 fat fillets from each fish (or ask the fishmonger to do this). Remove the tiny bones running along the centre of each fillet with tweezers.

2. For the celeriac, peel it with a knife. Cut it into 2.5 cm/1 inch cubes then boil until tender in salted water (about 15 minutes). Mash the celeriac with a potato masher, or press it through a sieve. Stir in the crème fraîche, half the olive oil and salt and pepper. The result should be a light, slightly runny purée.

3. For the lemons, pare the zest with a small zesting knife. Put the strips of lemon zest into a small bowl and squeeze the juice on top. Let this macerate for an hour then lift out with a slotted spoon. Half-fill a small frying pan with cooking oil, then, when hot, drop the zest into the oil. Have another small frying pan ready: after only a few seconds, pour the zest and hot oil through a metal sieve into the second (cold) pan. This way, the sieve catches the cooked zest.

4. Brush the mullet fillets with a little oil and season the skin sides with salt. Lay the fillets on a tray and grill under a high heat, through the skin side only. (This should take about 5–10 minutes, depending on the power of the grill).

5. To finish, spoon some celeriac on to 4 warmed plates. Dress the fish with lemon juice and lift it on to the purée. Drizzle a thread of olive oil along the edge of the plate and scatter deep-fried lemon zest over the top.

Menu

*G*oat's Cheese & Red Pepper Tart

*S*almon with Aioli and Cabbage

*G*ooseberry Streusel Cake
with Elderflower Cream

Seventeen

A THEME IN THIS MENU LIES IN THE USE OF INGREDIENTS WITH DISTINCTIVE flavours, which are cooked in a very simple manner. The tart has a light short pastry base and a gooey, creamy filling, topped with skinned red peppers. The salmon is roasted in a very hot oven, then served on a bed of stir-fried cabbage, with a simple garlic mayonnaise. The dessert is a gooseberry cake with a crumbly topping, served with a fragrant elderflower cream.

Many people have an innate aversion to goat's cheese. This tart, however, seems to please absolutely everyone, as it is served straight from the oven: the cheese is meltingly soft and the 'goaty' flavour less pronounced because the cheese is hot. I like to use a fairly mature cheese, such as Somerset goat's cheeses or Crottins de Chavignol. To grill the peppers, cut them into quarters, remove the seeds, then grill them until the skins are charred and black. Wrap them in foil for about half an hour, then remove the skins, by simply peeling away. Not only are these peppers softer and more digestible than raw ones, the grilling also imparts a faint smoky taste which goes well with the earthy flavour of the cheese. Another good idea for using skinned peppers is to cut them into slivers (use different colours) and toss them in a salad bowl with olive oil, black olives and capers, for a wonderfully bright, tasty salad.

For the salmon, ask your fishmonger for middle-cut fillets, and make sure the pin bones are removed. Whether you buy wild salmon during its season (the end of February to September) or farmed salmon (which has the advantage of being available all year), the style of cooking the fish ensures the flesh remains succulent, moist and firm. The oven temperature is very hot indeed, so be sure to preheat the oven well in advance – I give mine about an hour. By cooking for a very short time at a high temperature, the flesh does not have time to dry out. The aïoli is not too garlic-laden, for the garlic should only be a suggestion, or it will overpower the salmon. The cabbage is quickly stir-fried, in order to retain its crunchy texture. It is flavoured with *nam pla*, which is a fish sauce used frequently in South-East

Asian cookery. This clear thin sauce made from fermented salted fish is used to add a strong savoury taste which gives depth to any fish, meat, vegetable or egg dish. A simple Thai omelette is made with eggs mixed with *nam pla*; the result is simply stronger and slightly saltier, not at all fishy – you have to use a large amount of *nam pla* for a strongly fishy taste. In Thailand, it is a form of condiment, added after the cooking is finished, as we add salt and pepper. It is widely available in Asian food shops and from some supermarkets.

When we lived in Northern Germany, we sampled many different 'streusel' cakes, with their crumble-type topping. We had plum, cherry and apricot cakes, but I like it made with gooseberries. Gooseberries and elderflowers always make a wonderful combination, so the cake is delicious served warm with some elderflower cream. The cream is a mixture of Greek yoghurt (you could use whipped cream) and elderflower syrup. Although there are many commercial syrups available, home-made is not difficult to do. Cover freshly cut elderflowers with water in a large saucepan. Bring to the boil and simmer for 15–20 minutes, then strain into a measuring jug. For every 900 ml/$1\frac{1}{2}$ pints of liquid, add 500 g/1 lb sugar. Bring this slowly to the boil again (stirring to dissolve the sugar) and then boil fiercely for 5 minutes, before pouring into heatproof jugs, to cool. Pour into bottles, seal tightly and store in a cool place. You can also make a muscat grape-flavoured ice-cream, to accompany stewed gooseberries or rhubarb, by freezing the elderflower cream mixture in an ice-cream machine.

ADVANCE PREPARATION

You can bake the pastry blind in advance, but the filling should be cooked at the last minute. The aïoli can be made a couple of hours before, but the salmon and cabbage must be freshly cooked. The cake can be baked earlier and reheated, and the cream made in advance but removed from the fridge an hour before eating.

WINE SUGGESTIONS

Again, to accompany the goat's cheese you may wish to serve Sancerre. With the salmon and the aïoli, however, serve Verdicchio, which can also be served with the first course. A Riesling Auslese not only reinforces the Germanic overtones of the streusel cake, but it also complements the elderflower taste with a similar bouquet of its own.

Goat's Cheese and Red Pepper Tart

SERVES 6 AS A STARTER

FOR THE PASTRY

275 g/9 oz plain flour, sifted
$\frac{3}{4}$ tsp salt
150 g/5 oz unsalted butter, diced
1 egg
1 tbsp olive oil

FOR THE FILLING

200g–250 g/7–8 oz goat's cheese, rind removed,
 diced
200 ml/7 fl oz double cream
3 eggs, beaten
2 red peppers, cut into quarters, deseeded, grilled,
 skinned
freshly ground black pepper

1. For the pastry, place the flour, salt and butter in a food processor. Process until the mixture resembles breadcrumbs. Then slowly add the egg mixed with the oil, through the feeder tube, until the mixture forms a ball. Wrap with clingfilm and refrigerate for at least an hour.

2. Roll out the pastry to fit a 23 cm/9inch flan tin (preferably with a loose bottom). Prick the base with a fork, then chill the tin in the fridge for at least 30 minutes (or overnight).

3. Preheat the oven to Gas 6/200°C/400°F. Bake the pastry blind (lined with foil and baking beans) for 10 minutes, then remove the foil and beans and bake for a further 5 minutes.

4. Allow the pastry to cool, and reduce the oven to Gas 5/190°C/375°F.

5. For the filling, crumble the goat's cheese into the cooled pastry case. Cut the red pepper into thin slivers and arrange, like spokes of a wheel, on top of the cheese.

6. Whisk together the cream and egg, with plenty of freshly ground black pepper. (If the cheese is salty, add no salt at all.) Pour this over the tart and bake in the preheated oven for 25–35 minutes, until it is puffed up and golden brown. Let it rest for 10 minutes, then cut it into wedges and serve hot.

THE TART SHOULD NOT BE FROZEN

Salmon with Aïoli and Cabbage

FOR THE AÏOLI

2 large garlic cloves, peeled, crushed
a pinch of salt
1 egg
1 tbsp fresh lemon juice
75 ml/3 fl oz sunflower oil
125/150 ml/4–5 fl oz extra virgin olive oil

FOR THE FISH

4 middle-cut fillets of salmon (about 200g/7 oz
    each), pin bones removed (use tweezers or ask
    your fishmonger to do this)
olive oil, to brush
sea salt

FOR THE CABBAGE

$1\frac{1}{2}$ tbsp sunflower oil
$\frac{1}{2}$–1 tbsp *nam pla*
1 garlic clove, peeled crushed
1 small leek, cleaned, thinly sliced
$\frac{1}{2}$ white cabbage (about 375–400 g/12–13oz), very
    thinly sliced

1. For the aïoli, place the garlic and salt in a food processor, with the egg. Process for about 30 seconds. Add the lemon juice and process for another few seconds. Then, with the machine running, very slowly pour in the sunflower oil, then sufficient olive oil to achieve the consistency of mayonnaise. Taste, then add salt and lemon juice if necessary.

2. For the salmon, preheat the oven (well in advance!) to Gas 9/240°C/ 475°F. Remove the salmon from the fridge 30 minutes before cooking, then place on an oiled baking tray. Lightly brush with olive oil, then sprinkle with a little sea salt. Cook in the middle of the preheated oven for 7–8 minutes, then remove and let the fish rest for 3–4 minutes. (Check with the tip of a knife to see if the fish is cooked.)

3. For the cabbage, heat the oil in a large frying pan or wok; then, when it is very hot, add the *nam pla*. Stand back – it will splatter! Quickly add the garlic and leek, then cook for 1 minute. Add the cabbage and stir-fry for about 5 minutes, until the cabbage is just cooked, but still crunchy. Taste for seasoning and serve piping hot.

4. To serve, place a couple of spoonfuls of cabbage on to the middle of each warm plate. Place the salmon on top, then drizzle over the aïoli.

NONE OF THE MAIN COURSE CAN BE FROZEN

189

Gooseberry Streusel Cake with Elderflower Cream

SERVES 8

300 g/10 oz gooseberries, topped, tailed
25 g/1 oz caster sugar
2 tbsp Muscat dessert wine
175 g/6 oz plain flour, sifted
50 g/2 oz ground almonds
125 g/4 oz caster sugar
1 tsp baking powder
a pinch of salt
125 g/4 oz unsalted butter, chilled, diced
1 large egg, beaten

FOR THE ELDERFLOWER CREAM

3–4 tbsp thick Greek yoghurt
3–4 tsp elderflower syrup (amount depends on
    whether it is home-made)
a squeeze of fresh lemon juice

1. Cook the gooseberries with the 25 g/1 oz sugar and the Muscat wine, for 10–15 minutes, until just tender. Drain well, reserving the liquid.

2. Place the reserved juices into a saucepan and bring to the boil. Reduce the juices to about half, then pour these over the fruit. Leave to cool.

3. Place the flour, almonds, sugar, baking powder and salt in a food processor. Add the butter and process until it resembles breadcrumbs. With the machine running, add the egg to the mixture.

4. Preheat the oven to Gas 4/180°C/350°F. Line and butter a loose-bottom 20 cm/8 inch cake tin, then press in half of the cake mixture. The mixture should cover the base and go a little way up the sides.

190

5. Using a slotted spoon, spoon the gooseberries over the base, then sprinkle over the remaining cake mixture, as you would a crumble topping.

6. Bake in the middle of the preheated oven for about an hour, until golden brown. Let it rest for about 15 minutes, then remove from the tin. Dust with icing sugar and serve warm, with the cream.

7. For the cream, combine all the ingredients together, tasting to see how much elderflower syrup should be added (some commercial ones are very sweet.)

THE CAKE FREEZES SUCCESSFULLY. DO NOT FREEZE THE CREAM

The McCOY BROTHERS opened their restaurant in Staddlebridge, Yorkshire, in 1976. Since then, Eugene, Peter and Tom's skills as host and chefs are legendary, both in Yorkshire and throughout Britain. Genuine, informal hospitality is their trademark. Renowned for its accomplished cooking and its use of the best-quality ingredients, McCoy's restaurant is not only hugely successful, but it is also much admired for its great sense of style. Eugene's recipe is for salmon with cucumber and mint dressing – simplicity itself.

Salmon with Cucumber and Mint Dressing

¼ plus 1 whole cucumber
1 large sprig of mint
150 ml/5 fl oz vegetable stock
125 ml/4 fl oz double cream
25 g/1 oz unsalted butter
salt, pepper
4 × 175 g/6 oz pieces of salmon fillets, skinned

1. Liquidise and strain the quarter cucumber with the mint leaves. Remove to a saucepan, then heat, and reduce the liquid by half. Add the vegetables stock, then simmer to reduce the liquid by half.

2. Heat the double cream and simmer to reduce to half. Add it to the cucumber and mint liquid, and gradually whisk in the butter to thicken it. Season to taste.

3. Grill the salmon under a hot grill, in a bain-marie, for 4–5 minutes.

4. Peel and deseed the whole cucumber, cut it into 10 cm/4 inch batons. Blanch these in boiling water for 2 minutes, then drain well. Serve the salmon on warmed plates, with the cucumber batons piled on top, and the sauce spooned all around.

GOOSEBERRY STREUSEL CAKE

ROAST LEEKS

Eighteen

THIS FINAL MENU HAS NO STRIDENT COMBINATIONS OF FLAVOUR, YET HAS an unusual element to each course. The buckwheat bread to accompany the smoked trout and avocado starter tastes rather nutty and rich. The pheasant is cooked with a sauce which is flavoured with one of my favourite herbs, lovage. The simple accompaniment of parmesan-topped leeks allows plenty of room for a warm, comforting pudding, which is a combination of apple pie and pear crumble: the result is that you please everyone all of the time!

The use of buckwheat in bread is not common in Britain. It is frequently eaten in Russia, in the little yeast-raised pancakes – blinis – which are quite delicious topped with smetana (a type of sour cream), smoked salmon or caviar and washed down by ice-cold vodka. Like rye and barley flours, it should be mixed with high-gluten strong wheat flour, for successful breadmaking. The salad is made of ripe avocado and smoked trout, which go well with the savoury, almost smoky taste of the bread. Smoked trout resembles smoked salmon in taste and appearance, but is rather cheaper because of the increase in trout farms all over the country. The salad dressing is predominantly sour cream (continuing the blini theme), mixed with balsamic vinegar and freshly chopped chives.

As the pheasants are roasted in a hot oven for a comparatively short time, it is important to buy young birds. Overcooking pheasants can result in their flesh drying out, so baste them frequently with hot fat and remember to let them rest for at least ten minutes, which means the meat becomes less pink and more succulent. Celery and pheasant are a classic combination. As the taste of lovage is reminiscent of celery with a hint of lemon, I think it works very well in the buttery sauce. As a culinary herb, lovage has a long history, having been used by the Greeks and Romans and also in Britain, particularly in Scotland, where it still grows wild. Lovage is a very large perennial, which tends to dominate other herbs in a herb garden, but since you can also use the stems (peel them, boil lightly and serve in salads or with a white sauce), they are value for money! The

Menu

Buckwheat Bread with Smoked Trout
and Avocado Salad

Pheasant with Lovage
Roast Leeks

Apple and Pear Crumble Pie

accompanying leeks are roasted in a hot oven, with a topping of parmesan and olive oil. This would also make a delicious vegetarian dish, with a crowning of ratatouille or strong blue cheese such as Stilton, or the sheep's milk cheese, Lanark Blue.

The pudding has a rich butter pastry base, with an apple, pear and cinnamon filling, and a crumble topping made even crunchier with the addition of oats. If you are making this in the autumn, throw in a few wild brambles to the filling or some peeled, very finely chopped quince. In many sweet dishes – certainly cakes, biscuits or pies – it is usual to use ground cinnamon rather than cinnamon sticks. Spices should preferably be freshly ground, or, if bought ready-ground, used quickly, as their delicate flavour often becomes stale if kept too long. I like to serve this old-fashioned pudding with either thick Greek yoghurt, or cream whipped with just a dash of Poire William eau-de-vie.

ADVANCE PREPARATION

The bread can be made in advance and reheated. The salad should be prepared just before eating. All the main course should be cooked at the last minute. The pudding is best freshly baked, but, if necessary, can be reheated.

WINE SUGGESTIONS

To start with, serve a New Zealand Sauvignon Blanc (Cloudy Bay, Montana Marlborough). The pheasant with lovage has an intense savoury taste which requires a full-bodied red: try a Californian or Australian Pinot Noir. With the pudding serve a sweet Californian Gewurtztraminer, or an Australian Riesling.

Buckwheat Bread

400 g/13 oz strong white flour
75 g/3 oz buckwheat flour
1 tsp salt
1 tsp fast-action dried yeast (easy-blend)
2 tbsp plus 2 tsp olive oil
250–300 ml/8–10 fl oz tepid water

1. Place the flours, salt and yeast in bowl and mix together. Make a well in the centre and add 2 tbsp olive oil and sufficient tepid water to form a soft dough.

2. Turn the dough on to a floured board and knead for about 10 minutes, until smooth and elastic.

3. Place in a lightly oiled bowl, cover and let it rise in a warm place for about an hour. Then knock back the dough, divide it into 2 oval-shaped loaves and place on 2 oiled baking sheets. Brush the tops with 1 tsp olive oil and let the loaves rest in a warm place for half an hour.

4. Preheat the oven to Gas 7/220°C/425°F. Bake the loaves in the hot oven for about 15–20 minutes, until puffed up and golden brown.

5. Brush the tops with the remaining 1 tsp oil, and allow to cool slightly before cutting and serving warm with the salad.

Smoked Trout and Avocado Salad

2 ripe avocados
125–175 g/4–6 oz smoked trout slices
freshly ground black pepper
the juice of $\frac{1}{2}$ lemon

FOR THE DRESSING

100 ml/$3\frac{1}{2}$ fl oz sour cream
2 tbsp natural yoghurt
1 tbsp balsamic vinegar
$\frac{1}{2}$ tbsp freshly chopped basil
1 tbsp freshly chopped chives
salt, pepper

TO SERVE

1 tbsp freshly chopped chives

1. Peel the avocados and cut into quarters (or thick slices if they are large). Wrap slices of the smoked trout around each slice and lay these on a plate. Grind over the pepper, then squeeze over the lemon juice.

2. For the dressing, mix together all the dressing ingredients in a food processor or in a bowl with a whisk; taste for seasoning.

3. Spoon a little of the dressing over the trout-wrapped avocado. Sprinkle generously with the chopped chives. Serve at room temperature with the warm bread.

ONLY THE BREAD FREEZES WELL

Pheasant with Lovage

2 young pheasant (about 875 g/1¾ lb each), ready
  for the oven
40 g/1½ oz unsalted butter
175 ml/6 fl oz reduced pheasant (or dark chicken)
  stock
125 ml/4 fl oz dry white wine
a small handful of lovage leaves, chopped
75 g/3 oz unsalted butter, chilled, cubed
salt, pepper

TO SERVE

4 sprigs of fresh lovage

1. Cut each pheasant into 4 joints each (or ask your butcher to do this). Preheat the oven to Gas 7/220°C/425°F.

2. Heat the 40 g/1½ oz butter in a frying pan, then brown the pheasant joints (in 2 batches) all over.

3. Place the pheasant joints into a baking dish and pour over the juices from the pan. Roast in the preheated oven for 10 minutes; remove, cover them with foil and let them rest for 10–15 minutes.

4. Meanwhile, make the sauce: deglaze the baking dish over a direct heat, by adding the stock and stirring to scrape up all the caramelised bits. Over a high heat, boil until the liquid is reduced to about half. Strain into a clean saucepan.

5. Add the wine and lovage, then bring to the boil and simmer until the liquid is reduced to about two-thirds. Reduce the heat and gradually beat in the cubed butter, whisking after each piece is added. Season to taste with salt and pepper (adding more lovage if you think the flavour is not strong enough).

6. To serve, place the pheasant pieces on warmed serving plates, pour over a little of the sauce and decorate with some fresh lovage.

Roast Leeks

4 leeks, washed, trimmed
4 tbsp extra virgin olive oil
25 g/1 oz freshly grated parmesan

TO SERVE

freshly ground black pepper

1. Preheat the oven to Gas 5/190°C/375°F. Slice the leeks in half lengthwise, then cut in half if they are very long. Oil a baking dish with 1 tbsp of the oil and lay in the leeks, side by side, the cut side up.

2. Slowly drizzle over the remaining oil (letting it seep into all the layers of leek). Sprinkle with the parmesan.

3. Bake them uncovered in the preheated oven for about 30 minutes, basting often with the oil. (You can start this before you put in the pheasant, then place the leeks at the bottom of the oven when you increase the oven temperature for the pheasant.)

4. Remove from the oven, grind over some black pepper and serve them in their dish, piping hot.

NONE OF THE MAIN COURSE CAN BE FROZEN

Apple and Pear Crumble Pie

FOR THE PASTRY

125 g/4 oz plain flour, sifted
a pinch of salt
1 tsp caster sugar
65 g/2½ oz unsalted butter, chilled, cubed
1 egg, beaten

FOR THE FILLING

2 large cooking apples, peeled, finely sliced
1 large pear, peeled, finely sliced
25 g/1 oz caster sugar
1 tsp cinnamon
¼ tsp mace
25 g/1 oz butter

FOR THE CRUMBLE

75 g/3 oz unsalted butter, chilled, cubed
50 g/2 oz plain flour, sifted
75 g/3 oz soft dark brown sugar
75 g/3 oz porridge oats

TO SERVE

Greek yoghurt or double cream
Poire Williem eau-de-vie, optional

1. For the pastry, mix the flour, salt and sugar in a food processor. Add the butter and process until it resembles breadcrumbs. Add the egg and process briefly, until it comes together as a ball. Wrap in clingfilm and chill for 30 minutes.

2. Roll out the pastry to a 20 cm/8 inch pie plate and refrigerate for an hour.

3. Preheat the oven to Gas 5/190°C/375°F.

4. For the filling, mix the apples, pear, sugar, cinnamon and mace together, then spoon on to the pastry base. Dot with the butter.

5. For the crumble, mix together the butter and flour in a food processor, (or rub in, by hand) then remove to a bowl and add the sugar and oats, so it forms a crumble mixture. Spoon this over the filling, pressing carefully, so it is all covered.

6. Place on a baking tray (juices might seep out) and bake in the preheated oven for 45 minutes.

7. Serve warm, in wedges, with Greek yoghurt or cream whipped with 1 tsp Poire Williem eau-de-vie.

THE PIE FREEZES SUCCESSFULLY, AND SHOULD BE REHEATED IN
A WARM OVEN, TO SERVE

ANTON EDELMANN started his apprenticeship as a chef in a small village in Bavaria. After subsequently working in various restaurants in many European cities, he came to the Savoy Hotel in 1982, where he is Maître Chef des Cuisines and also a director. His accomplished, creative and sophisticated style of cooking has inspired many younger chefs; he has a staff of a hundred working in his kitchen. Anton very kindly shares one of his exquisite dessert recipes – apple wrapped in pastry with a Calvados butter.

Apples Wrapped in Pastry with Calvados Butter Sauce

75 g/3 oz sultanas
25 ml/1 fl oz Calvados
4 Reinette apples
ground cinnamon
300 g/10 oz puff pastry
1 egg yolk, beaten
25 g/1 oz icing sugar
50 g/2 oz caster sugar
50 ml/2 fl oz water
10 g/$\frac{1}{4}$ oz glucose
50 g/2 oz unsalted butter
150 ml/5 fl oz double cream

1. Soak the sultanas in the Calvados for 1 hour. Drain, reserving the Calvados. Top and tail the apples, so they stand level. Sprinkle the sultanas with the cinnamon and use to fill the centre of each apple.

2. Roll out the puff pastry to 3 mm/$\frac{1}{8}$ inch thick. Cut out 4 ovals (about 18 × 13 cm/7 × 5 inches) and brush the edges with egg yolk. Preheat the oven to Gas 5/190°C/375°F.

3. Enclose an apple in each oval and seal the edges well. Crimp with a small knife. Brush each one with egg yolk and make a small cut in the top. Bake

in the preheated oven for about 20 minutes. Remove from the oven and dust generously with icing sugar. Place under a hot grill to give a nice shiny glaze.

4. For the Calvados butter sauce, cook the caster sugar, water and glucose in a heavy-based saucepan until it is a pale amber colour. Stir in the butter and the cream, reserving 25 ml/1 fl oz of the cream. Add the reserved Calvados.

5. To serve, position each apple on a warm plate and surround with the sauce. Feather with the reserved cream.

Chefs' Addresses

ALBERT ROUX, Maître Cuisinier de France, Le Gavroche Restaurant, 43 Upper Brook Street, London

CLIVE HOWE, The Lygon Arms, Broadway, Worcestershire

RICK STEIN, The Seafood Restaurant, Riverside, Padstow, Cornwall

ANTHONY TOBIN, South Lodge Hotel, Lower Beeding, West Sussex

GARY RHODES, The Greenhouse, 27A Hay's Mews, London

CHRISTOPHER CHOWN, Plas Bodegroes, Pwllheli, North Wales

ANTONY WORRALL THOMPSON, 190 Queen's Gate, London

BETTY ALLEN, The Airds Hotel, Port Appin, Argyll

DAVID ADLARD, Adlard's Restaurant, 79 Upper St Giles Street, Norwich

PAUL RANKINE, Roscoff Restaurant, Shaftesbury Square, Belfast

JOHN TOVEY, Miller Howe, Windermere, Cumbria

ALASTAIR LITTLE, Alastair Little Restaurant, 49 Frith Street, London

PAUL HEATHCOTE, Heathcote's Restaurant, Longridge, Lancashire

BRIAN TURNER, Turner's, 87–89 Walton Street, London

NICK NAIRN, Braeval Old Mill, Aberfoyle, Stirlingshire

SHAUN HILL, Gidleigh Park, Chagford, Devon

EUGENE MCCOY, McCoy's Restaurant, The Tontine, Staddlebridge, North Yorkshire

ANTON EDELMANN, Maître Chef des Cuisines, The Savoy Hotel, London

Index